100 BEST-EVER STEP-BY-STEP BARBECUES

The ultimate guide to grilling in 340 stunning photographs with recipes for appetizers, fish, meat, vegetables, relishes, sauces and desserts

Edited by JAN CUTLER

southwater

This edition is published by Southwater, an imprint of Anness Publishing Ltd,
108 Great Russell Street, London WC1B 3NA; info@anness.com

www.southwaterbooks.com; www.annesspublishing.com; twitter: @Anness_Books

If you like the images in this book and would like to investigate using them for publishing, promotions or advertising,
please visit our website www.practicalpictures.com for more information.

© Anness Publishing Ltd 2015

A CIP catalogue record for this book is available from the British Library.

Publisher: Joanna Lorenz
Editorial Director: Helen Sudell
Editors: Catherine Stuart and Elizabeth Woodland
Contributing Editor: Linda Tubby
Production Controller: Rosanna Anness
Design: Adelle Morris and Diane Pullen

COOK'S NOTES
Bracketed terms are intended for American readers.
For all recipes, quantities are given in both metric and imperial measures and, where appropriate, in standard cups and spoons.
Follow one set of measures, but not a mixture, because they are not interchangeable.
Standard spoon and cup measures are level. 1 tsp = 5ml, 1 tbsp = 15ml, 1 cup = 250ml/8fl oz.
Australian standard tablespoons are 20ml. Australian readers should use 3 tsp in place of 1 tbsp for measuring small quantities.
American pints are 16fl oz/2 cups. American readers should use 20fl oz/2.5 cups in place of 1 pint when measuring liquids.
Electric oven temperatures in this book are for conventional ovens. When using a fan oven, the temperature will probably need to be reduced
by about 10–20°C/20–40°F. Since ovens vary, you should check with your manufacturer's instruction book for guidance.
The nutritional analysis given for each recipe is calculated per portion (i.e. serving or item), unless otherwise stated. If the recipe gives a range,
such as Serves 4–6, then the nutritional analysis will be for the smaller portion size, i.e. 6 servings. The analysis does not include
optional ingredients, such as salt added to taste.
Medium (US large) eggs are used unless otherwise stated.

PUBLISHER'S NOTE
Although the advice and information in this book are believed to be accurate and true at the time of going to press, neither the authors
nor the publisher can accept any legal responsibility or liability for any errors or omissions that may have been made nor for
any inaccuracies nor for any loss, harm or injury that comes about from following instructions or advice in this book.

Main front cover image shows Fish Brochettes with Peperonata – for recipe, see page 42

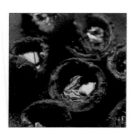

BEST-EVER STEP-BY-STEP
100 BARBECUES

  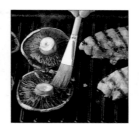 

CONTENTS

 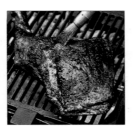  

INTRODUCTION

barbecue today: sitting together and chatting, surrounded by the aroma of food cooking over open coals. And because the juices of barbecued food drip on to the coals and form aromatic smoke, it has that special, taste-bud-tingling smell. Indeed, the smell is so delicious and outdoor eating so enjoyable that it really stimulates the appetite, so when catering for a barbecue, cook plenty!

MODERN BARBECUES

Barbecuing techniques have changed over the years and modern barbecues, too, have made cooking more efficient. The kettle barbecue, for example, has a lid and this helps to create an even temperature for cooking small items of food as well as whole joints. Barbecues can also have spits, and these days if you don't want to get messy with the charcoal you can use a gas or electric barbecue, which are available in a variety of sizes.

DISCOVERING BARBECUE STYLE

A barbecue can be a wonderfully spontaneous affair with food quickly prepared and cooked. Choose straightforward recipes, perhaps using the griddle, for that fast, fun and no-

Below: Use aromatic wood to add a smoky flavour to barbecued foods.

The sun is shining, the weather is warm and you feel like eating outside – it's got to be a barbecue! There's nothing quite like *al fresco* eating, especially if the food is cooked over an open fire. A barbecue is a comfortable and sociable affair, loved by children and adults alike, and can be just as delightful at home in the garden, in the countryside or on the beach.

TRACING ITS ROOTS

No one is certain where the term "barbecue" actually began, but it probably derived from the Spanish word *barbacoa* in the mid-17th century, which originally meant "a wooden frame on posts". This might have been equipment for smoking meat, and it is believed that the Caribbean Arawak Indians taught the Spanish sailors the art of smoking meat in this way.

Barbecuing has certainly been popular in America for a long time. Even before the Civil War, people in the South were roasting pigs outdoors at social gatherings. In the 1800s the cowboys on the cattle ranches cooked tougher cuts of meat for several hours over an open fire, and during the 19th century churches, political rallies and parties were using the barbecue as a great way to get people together. But, over the years, even in cooler climes,

Above: For tasty little snacks, combine minced meat with herbs and nuts, shape into balls and grill on sticks.

the barbecue has become one of the exciting things about summer – eating outside in the warm air, getting together with other people and being sociable. If you are eating with your family, this is a time when everyone feels involved, even if the kids are playing and running outside while the adults cook and enjoy a long, relaxing drink.

Also, because barbecues come in all sizes and to suit all pockets, there's one for every situation, so you can cook outside even if you have a fairly small space, as long as you are careful not to site the barbecue unsafely, such as under a garage door or a carport or within 3m/10ft of the house.

Of course, cooking over an open fire goes back to our ancestors' distant past and is still an essential part of the culinary cultures of countries all over the world. In hotter climes daily cooking takes place outdoors for a variety of reasons, especially because the heat (as well as the smoke) makes it unbearable to cook inside. Once cooking is transferred outside it takes on a completely different appeal; it becomes sociable and that's probably the most important aspect of the fuss barbecue. Griddles are also ideal for the spontaneous barbecue, and for a first course or for nibbles, so that the main course can be cooked when the heat is less fierce. Tips and techniques like these are explained in the book.

If you are catering for larger numbers of people, careful planning will ensure everything runs smoothly. Have all the preparation completed in advance, and if you are cooking away from home everything will need to be easily transportable to the picnic site. Make sure you have plenty of equipment for carrying raw food (as well as keeping it cool) and clean equipment for the food once cooked. Keep a griddle on hand if possible: it is not just a rainy weather substitute, but an ideal platform for cooking foods when coals are very hot.

BE ADVENTUROUS

Once you learn how versatile your barbecue can be, you can enjoy a world of different flavours and textures. Not only can you cook up your favourite burgers and other quick, simple but nevertheless delicious meals, but you can also create tasty kebabs, steaks, parcels of fish wrapped in leaves or foil, whole chickens and also griddled main courses or side dishes of meat, fish and

Below: Sprigs of herbs can be smoked over coals to add extra flavour.

vegetables – flavoured in all kinds of different ways! And if you want to stay healthy and keep trim for the summer, barbecued food can be made healthy and low in fat simply by replacing oily marinades with low-fat ones and misting with oil, and by using lean meat or fish.

Above: Chargrilled vegetables are an ideal addition to cooked salads.

The other great thing about all the barbecue recipes in this book is that they can be cooked indoors under a grill (broiler), in the oven, or over the hob, so you can try some of the hearty barbecued dishes in the winter too. Of course, you must never cook with a barbecue indoors unless it is specially designed for this purpose, as are some electric barbecues.

Use this book to help you choose the right barbecue for the right occasion, and to understand the basics of setting up and cooking. By trying out and sampling the many mouthwatering dishes on the following pages, you will become a truly versatile cook, able to experiment with new flavours and to present the food beautifully. Recipes from all over the world are included, and many have helpful tips, ensuring that you have as much information at your fingertips as possible to ensure that your barbecue is a success.

APPETIZERS AND LIGHT BITES

As soon as the barbecue is set alight, appetites awaken and everyone gets ready to enjoy some exceptionally flavourful food. So don't keep those hungry people waiting — whip up a selection of exciting and adventurous nibbles and appetizers. Many of the recipes in this chapter use the griddle, which can be placed over coals that are too hot for cooking most foods direct on the grill rack, and is therefore ideal for use during the first flush of heat from the barbecue. You will be surprised at the variety of foods that you can cook on the barbecue, from mini burgers to griddled corn cakes and tender morsels of meat mounted on sticks, plus quickly cooked shellfish that needs hardly any preparation. And remember that many of these light bites can also be included on the side as part of a main course, or are simply perfect as party food.

CORN TOSTADITAS <u>WITH</u> SALSA

THIS IS JUST THE RIGHT SNACK OR APPETIZER TO COOK WHEN THE COALS ARE VERY HOT, AS IT USES A GRIDDLE. THE SALSA AND GUACAMOLE ARE QUICK TO PREPARE AND TASTE WONDERFUL WITH THE STRIPY TOSTADITAS. MAKE SURE THE GRIDDLE HAS HEATED UP WELL BEFORE YOU ADD THE TOSTADITAS.

SERVES SIX

INGREDIENTS
  30ml/2 tbsp chipotle or
    other chilli oil
  15ml/1 tbsp sunflower oil
  8 yellow corn tortillas, about
    300g/11oz total weight
For the salsa
  4 tomatoes
  30ml/2 tbsp chopped fresh basil
  juice of ½ lime
  20ml/4 tsp good quality sweet
    chilli sauce
  1 small red onion, finely chopped
    (optional)
  salt and ground black pepper
For the guacamole
  4 avocados
  juice of ½ lime
  1 fresh fat mild chilli, seeded and
    finely chopped
  salt and ground black pepper

1 Make the salsa 1 or 2 hours ahead if possible, to allow the flavours to blend. Cut the tomatoes in half, remove the cores and scoop out most of the seeds. Dice the flesh. Add the chopped basil, lime juice and sweet chilli sauce. Stir in the onion, if using, then add salt and pepper to taste.

2 To make the guacamole, cut the avocados in half, prize out the stones (pits), then scoop the flesh into a bowl. Add the lime juice, chopped chilli and seasoning. Mash with a fork to a fairly rough texture. Prepare the barbecue.

3 Mix the chilli and sunflower oils together. Stack the tortillas on a board. Lift the first tortilla off the stack and brush it lightly with the oil mixture. Turn it over and place it on the board, then brush the top with oil. Repeat with the other tortillas to produce a new stack.

4 Slice this stack of tortillas diagonally to produce six fat triangles. Heat the griddle on the grill rack over hot coals. Peel off a few tostaditas to griddle for 30 seconds on each side, pressing each one down lightly into the ridges.

5 Transfer the tostaditas to a bowl, so that they are supported by its sides. As they cool, they will shape themselves to the curve of the bowl. Serve with the salsa and guacamole.

Energy 334kcal/1396kJ; Protein 5.6g; Carbohydrate 36.8g, of which sugars 6.3g; Fat 19.1g, of which saturates 3.6g; Cholesterol 0mg; Calcium 71mg; Fibre 4.4g; Sodium 313mg.

CROSTINI

THIS IS A GREAT WAY TO KEEP HUNGER PANGS AT BAY WHILE YOU WAIT FOR THE MAIN COURSE. AS SOON AS THE BARBECUE IS READY, SIMPLY GRILL THE SLICED BREAD, HEAP ON THE SAUCE AND DRIZZLE OVER PLENTY OF GOOD EXTRA VIRGIN OLIVE OIL.

SERVES SIX

INGREDIENTS
2 sfilatino (Italian bread sticks),
  sliced lengthways into 3 pieces
1 garlic clove, cut in half
leaves from 4 fresh oregano sprigs
18 Kalamata olives, slivered off
  their pits
extra virgin olive oil, for drizzling
ground black pepper
For the aromatic tomatoes
  800g/1¾lb ripe plum tomatoes
  30ml/2 tbsp extra virgin olive oil
  2 garlic cloves, crushed to a paste
    with a pinch of salt
  1 small piece of dried chilli, seeds
    removed, finely chopped

VARIATION
Baguettes or ciabatta bread, cut
diagonally to give long slices, will work
just as well as sfilatino.

1 Prepare the barbecue. To make the aromatic tomatoes, plunge the tomatoes into boiling water for 30 seconds, then refresh in cold water. Peel away the skins, remove the seeds and core and roughly chop the flesh. Mix the oil and crushed garlic in a large frying pan.

2 Place on the stove over a high heat. Once the garlic starts to sizzle, add the tomatoes and the chilli; do not let the garlic burn. Cook for 2 minutes. The aim is to evaporate the liquid rather than pulp the tomatoes, which should keep their shape.

3 Toast the bread on both sides either by laying it on the grill rack or by using a griddle. If you use the griddle, press the bread down with a spatula to produce the attractive stripes. Generously rub each slice with the cut side of a piece of garlic.

4 Roughly chop all but a few of the oregano leaves and mix them into the tomato sauce. Pile the mixture on to the toasted sfilatino. Scatter over the whole oregano leaves and the olive slivers. Sprinkle with plenty of pepper, drizzle with lots of olive oil and serve at once.

Energy 261kcal/1103kJ; Protein 7.8g; Carbohydrate 38.8g, of which sugars 6.2g; Fat 9.4g, of which saturates 1.4g; Cholesterol 0mg; Calcium 95mg; Fibre 3.1g; Sodium 558mg.

CORN GRIDDLE CAKES

KNOWN AS AREPAS, *THESE GRIDDLE CAKES ARE A STAPLE BREAD IN SEVERAL* LATIN AMERICAN *COUNTRIES. THEY ARE DELICIOUS FILLED WITH SOFT WHITE CHEESE, AS IN THIS RECIPE, OR SIMPLY EATEN PLAIN AS AN ACCOMPANIMENT. WITH THEIR CRISP CRUST AND CHEWY INTERIOR,* AREPAS *MAKE AN UNUSUAL AND TASTY SNACK OR ACCOMPANIMENT TO A BARBECUE MEAL.*

MAKES FIFTEEN

INGREDIENTS
200g/7oz/1¾ cups *masarepa* (or
    masa harina) (see Cook's Tip)
2.5ml/½ tsp salt
300ml/½ pint/1¼ cups water
15ml/1 tbsp oil
200g/7oz fresh white cheese, such
    as queso fresco or mozzarella,
    roughly chopped

1 Combine the *masarepa* or *masa harina* and salt in a bowl. Gradually stir in the measured water to make a soft dough, then set aside for about 20 minutes.

2 Divide the dough into 15 equal-sized balls, then, using your fingers, flatten each ball into a circle, approximately 1cm/½in thick. Prepare the barbecue.

3 Heat a large, heavy frying pan or flat griddle over a medium heat and add 5ml/1 tsp oil. Using a piece of kitchen paper, gently wipe the surface of the frying pan, leaving it just lightly greased.

4 Place five of the *arepas* in the frying pan or on the griddle. Cook for about 4 minutes, then flip over and cook for a further 4 minutes. The *arepas* should be lightly blistered on both sides.

5 Open the *arepas* and fill each with a few small pieces of fresh white cheese. Return to the pan to cook until the cheese begins to melt. Remove from the heat and keep warm.

6 Cook the remaining ten *arepas* in the same way, oiling the pan and wiping with kitchen paper in between batches, to ensure it is always lightly greased. Serve the arepas while still warm so that the melted cheese is soft and runny.

COOK'S TIP
Masarepa is a flour made with the white corn grown in the Andes. Look for it in Latin American food stores. If it is not available, replace it with *masa harina*, the flour used to make tamales. The result will not be quite as delicate, but the *arepas* will be equally delicious.

VARIATION
Instead of cheese, try a delicious beef filling. Simply fry some minced (ground) beef in oil in a frying pan with ½ chopped onion, 1 small red chilli, finely chopped, 1 crushed garlic clove, ground black pepper and fresh thyme. When thoroughly cooked, stuff the mixture inside the *arepas*.

Energy 86kcal/363kJ; Protein 3.7g; Carbohydrate 10.4g, of which sugars 0.2g; Fat 3.6g, of which saturates 2g; Cholesterol 8mg; Calcium 67mg; Fibre 0.4g; Sodium 53mg.

CLASSIC QUESADILLAS

THESE CHEESE-FILLED TORTILLAS ARE THE MEXICAN EQUIVALENT OF TOASTED SANDWICHES. SERVE
THEM HOT OR THEY WILL BECOME CHEWY. IF YOU ARE MAKING THEM FOR A CROWD, YOU COULD FILL
AND FOLD THE TORTILLAS IN ADVANCE THEN ADD THE CHILLI AND COOK THEM TO ORDER.

SERVES EIGHT

INGREDIENTS
   400g/14oz mozzarella,
     Monterey Jack or mild
     Cheddar cheese
   2 fresh Fresno chillies (optional)
   16 wheat flour tortillas, about
     15cm/6in across
   onion relish or tomato salsa,
     to serve

COOK'S TIP
It is best to put on protective gloves
before peeling the skin from the roasted
chillies. It is actually the membrane
attached to the seeds, rather than the
flesh, that emits the stinging toxins.

1 If using mozzarella cheese, it must be
drained thoroughly and then patted dry
and sliced into thin strips. Monterey
Jack and Cheddar cheese should both
be coarsely grated, as finely grated
cheese will melt and ooze away when
cooking. Set the cheese aside in a bowl.

2 Prepare the barbecue. If using the
chillies, spear them on a long-handled
metal skewer and roast them on the grill
rack over high heat or directly over a
flame until the skin blisters and
darkens. Do not let the flesh burn.
Place the roasted chillies in a plastic
bag and seal tightly or under an
upturned bowl. Set aside for 20 minutes
for the skin to loosen.

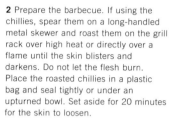

3 Remove the roasted chillies from the
bag and carefully peel off the skin. Cut
off the stalk, then slit the chillies and
scrape out all the seeds. Cut the flesh
into 16 even-sized thin strips.

4 Heat the griddle or a frying pan on
the grill rack over hot coals. Place one
tortilla on the griddle or pan at a time,
sprinkle about one sixteenth of the
cheese on to one half and add a strip of
chilli, if using. Fold the tortilla over the
cheese and press the edges together
gently to seal. Cook the filled tortilla for
1 minute, then turn over and cook the
other side for 1 minute.

5 Remove the filled tortilla from the
griddle or pan, cut it into three triangles
or four strips and serve immediately
while it is still hot, with the onion relish
or tomato salsa.

VARIATIONS
Try spreading a thin layer of your
favourite salsa on the tortillas before
adding the cheese, or add some cooked
chicken or prawns (shrimp) before
folding the tortillas.

Energy 392kcal/1645kJ; Protein 18.2g; Carbohydrate 44.8g, of which sugars 0.8g; Fat 16.8g, of which saturates 10.4g; Cholesterol 53mg; Calcium 428mg; Fibre 1.8g; Sodium 545mg.

SMOKY AUBERGINE ON CIABATTA

COOKING THE AUBERGINES WHOLE, OVER AN OPEN FLAME, GIVES THEM A DISTINCTIVE SMOKY FLAVOUR AND AROMA, AS WELL AS TENDER, CREAMY FLESH. COOK THEM WHEN THE HEAT IS FIERCE. THEY THEN NEED TO COOL FOR ABOUT 20 MINUTES BEFORE THEY ARE CHOPPED AND SERVED.

SERVES FOUR TO SIX

INGREDIENTS

2 aubergines (eggplants)
2 red (bell) peppers
3–5 garlic cloves, chopped, or more to taste
2.5ml/½ tsp ground cumin
juice of ½–1 lemon, to taste
2.5ml/½ tsp sherry or wine vinegar
45–60ml/3–4 tbsp extra virgin olive oil
1–2 shakes of cayenne pepper, Tabasco or other hot pepper sauce
coarse sea salt
chopped fresh coriander (cilantro), to garnish
pitta bread wedges or thinly sliced French bread or ciabatta bread, sesame seed crackers and cucumber slices, to serve

1 Prepare the barbecue. Place the aubergines and peppers over a medium-low heat on the grill rack (they can also be cooked inside). Turn the vegetables frequently until deflated and the skins are evenly charred.

2 Put the aubergines and peppers in a plastic bag and seal tightly or under an upturned bowl. Cool over 20 minutes.

3 Peel the vegetables, reserving the juices, and roughly chop the flesh. Put the flesh in a bowl and add the juices, garlic, cumin, lemon juice, vinegar, olive oil, hot pepper seasoning and salt. Mix well to combine. Turn the mixture into a serving bowl and garnish with coriander. Serve with bread, toasted on the barbecue, sesame seed crackers and cucumber slices.

Energy 95kcal/391kJ; Protein 1.3g; Carbohydrate 5g, of which sugars 4.7g; Fat 7.9g, of which saturates 1.2g; Cholesterol 0mg; Calcium 12mg; Fibre 2.5g; Sodium 4mg.

LITTLE COURGETTE WRAPS

THIS IS A TASTY FIRST COURSE OR VEGETABLE SIDE DISH USING MINI MOZZARELLA BALLS WRAPPED IN SUCCULENT STRIPS OF COURGETTES. ACCOMPANY WITH STRONGLY FLAVOURED SALAD LEAVES.

SERVES SIX

INGREDIENTS
    2 large yellow courgettes (zucchini),
      about 675g/1½lb total weight
    45ml/3 tbsp olive oil
    250g/9oz baby leaf spinach
    250g/9oz mini mozzarella balls
    salad burnet, rocket (arugula) and
      mizuna leaves, to garnish (optional)
For the dressing
    2 whole, unpeeled garlic cloves
    30ml/2 tbsp white wine vinegar
    30ml/2 tbsp olive oil
    15ml/1 tbsp extra virgin olive oil
    45ml/3 tbsp walnut oil
    salt and ground black pepper

COOK'S TIP
Sweeter than the popular green variety,
yellow courgettes are quite easy to find.

1 To make the dressing, place the garlic in a small pan with water to cover. Bring to the boil, lower the heat and simmer for 5 minutes. Drain. When cool enough to handle, pop the garlic cloves out of their skins and crush to a smooth paste with a little salt. Scrape into a bowl and add the vinegar. Whisk in the oils and season to taste.

2 Slice each courgette lengthways into six or more broad strips, about 3mm/⅛in wide. Lay them on a tray a little apart from each other. Set aside 5ml/1 tsp of the oil and brush the rest over the strips, making sure each one is evenly coated in the oil.

3 Place a wok over a high heat. When it starts to smoke, add the reserved oil and stir-fry the spinach for 30 seconds.

4 When the spinach is just beginning to wilt over the heat, tip it into a sieve and drain well, then pat the leaves dry with kitchen paper. Tear or slice the mozzarella balls in half and place on kitchen paper to drain.

5 Prepare the barbecue. Position a lightly oiled grill rack over medium-hot coals. Lay the courgettes on the rack. Grill on one side only for 2–3 minutes, or until striped golden. As each strip cooks, return it to the tray, grilled-side up.

6 Place small heaps of spinach towards one end of each courgette strip. Lay two pieces of mozzarella on each pile of spinach. Season well.

7 Using a metal spatula, carefully transfer the topped strips, a few at a time, back to the barbecue rack and grill for about 2 minutes, or until the underside of each is striped with golden-brown grill marks.

8 When the cheese starts to melt, fold the plain section of each courgette over the filling to make a wrap. Lift off carefully and drain on kitchen paper. Serve with the garnish of salad leaves, if you like, and drizzle the dressing over.

COOK'S TIP
You need large courgettes measuring about 19cm/7½in, to create good-sized wraps when cut into strips.

Energy 237kcal/977kJ; Protein 11g; Carbohydrate 2.7g, of which sugars 2.5g; Fat 20.2g, of which saturates 7.4g; Cholesterol 24mg; Calcium 250mg; Fibre 1.9g; Sodium 224mg.

GRILLED BABY ARTICHOKES

THIS IS AN ENJOYABLE WAY TO EAT ARTICHOKES. JUST HOLD THE SKEWER WITH THE ARTICHOKE IN ONE HAND, TEAR OFF A LEAF WITH THE OTHER AND DIP THAT INTO THE HOT MELTED BUTTER.

SERVES SIX

INGREDIENTS

   12 baby artichokes with stalks,
      about 1.3kg/3lb total weight
   1 lemon, halved
   200g/7oz/scant 1 cup butter
   2 garlic cloves, crushed with a pinch
      of salt
   15ml/1 tbsp chopped fresh flat
      leaf parsley
   salt and ground black pepper

1 Soak 12 wooden skewers in cold water for 30 minutes. Drain, then skewer a baby artichoke on to each one. Bring a large pan of salted water to the boil. Squeeze the juice of one lemon half, and add it, with the lemon shell, to the pan.

2 Place the artichokes head first into the pan and boil for 5–8 minutes, or until just tender. Drain well. Set aside for up to 1 hour or use at once.

3 Prepare the barbecue. Put the butter, garlic and parsley into a small pan and squeeze in the juice of the remaining half-lemon.

4 Position a lightly oiled grill rack over the coals to heat over medium heat. If the artichokes have been allowed to cool, wrap the heads in foil and place them on the grill for 3 minutes, then unwrap and return to the heat for 1 minute, turning frequently. If they are still hot, grill without the foil for 4 minutes, turning often.

5 When the artichokes are almost ready, melt the butter sauce in the pan on the barbecue. Either transfer the sauce to six small serving bowls or pour a little on to each plate. Serve it with the artichokes on their skewers.

COOK'S TIP
Have plenty of napkins on hand to catch any stray drops of butter sauce!

Energy 263kcal/1084kJ; Protein 1.4g; Carbohydrate 2.5g, of which sugars 1.2g; Fat 27.7g, of which saturates 17.4g; Cholesterol 71mg; Calcium 49mg; Fibre 1.4g; Sodium 262mg.

GRIDDLED CHEESE BITES

*THESE GRIDDLED CHEESE CUBES WRAPPED IN AROMATIC LEAVES ARE DELICIOUS WITH A COLD
RESINOUS WINE, PLENTY OF EXCELLENT OLIVES, FRUITY OLIVE OIL AND RUSTIC BREAD. THEY TAKE
ONLY MINUTES TO COOK AND MAKE THE PERFECT PRE-DINNER SNACK FOR A CROWD.*

SERVES SIX

INGREDIENTS

  18 large bay leaves or mixed bay and
    lemon leaves
  275g/10oz Kefalotiri or Kasseri
    cheese, cut into 18 cubes
  20ml/4 tsp extra virgin olive oil
  ground black pepper

1 Soak 18 short wooden skewers in cold
water for 30 minutes. Add the bay
and/or lemon leaves to the water to
prevent them from burning when
cooked in the griddle.

2 Put the cheese cubes in a dish large
enough to hold the skewers. Pour over
the olive oil. Sprinkle over a little pepper
and toss well. Drain the skewers, then
thread them with the cheese and
drained bay leaves and/or lemon leaves.
Put the skewers of cheese back in the
oil. Prepare the barbecue.

3 Heat the griddle on the grill rack over
hot coals. When hot, lower the heat a
little and place the skewers on the
griddle, evenly spacing them. Cook for
about 5 seconds on each side. The
pieces of cheese should have golden-
brown lines, and should just be starting
to melt. Serve immediately.

COOK'S TIP
Do try to get hold of the recommended
cheese, Kefalotiri, which is a mature
cheese with a sharp nutty flavour. It
originates from the island of Crete.

Energy 213kcal/880kJ; Protein 11.8g; Carbohydrate 0g, of which sugars 0g; Fat 18.4g, of which saturates 10.6g; Cholesterol 48mg; Calcium 316mg; Fibre 0g; Sodium 307mg.

FETA-STUFFED SQUID

HERE IS A FABULOUS RECIPE FROM GREECE THAT COMBINES TWO OF THE MOST POPULAR INGREDIENTS FROM THAT COUNTRY: SQUID AND FETA CHEESE. SCENTED WITH MARJORAM AND GARLIC, THE SQUID CONTAINS A CREAMY MARINATED FETA CHEESE FILLING. IT IS SIMPLE TO PREPARE AND QUICK TO COOK.

SERVES FOUR

INGREDIENTS
    4 medium squid, about 900g/2lb
       total weight, prepared
    4–8 finger-length slices of
       feta cheese
    lemon wedges, to serve
For the marinade
    90ml/6 tbsp olive oil
    2 garlic cloves, crushed
    3–4 fresh marjoram sprigs, leaves
       removed and chopped
    salt and ground black pepper

COOK'S TIP
Ask your fishmonger to prepare the squid for you so that the bodies are intact. He will sever the tentacles and the two side fins, which you can cook separately.

1 Rinse the squid thoroughly, inside and out, and drain well. Lay the squid bodies and tentacles in a shallow dish that will hold them in a single layer. Tuck the pieces of cheese between the squid.

2 To make the marinade, pour the oil into a jug (pitcher) or bowl and whisk in the garlic and marjoram. Season to taste with salt and pepper. Pour the marinade over the squid and the cheese, then cover and leave in a cool place to marinate for 2–3 hours, turning once. Soak four wooden skewers in water for 30 minutes.

3 Insert 1 or 2 pieces of cheese and a few pieces of marjoram from the marinade into each squid and thread the tentacles on skewers by piercing at the centre to hold them in place.

4 Prepare a barbecue. Position a lightly oiled grill rack over the hot coals. Grill the stuffed squid over medium heat for about 6 minutes, then turn them over carefully. Grill them for 1–2 minutes more, then add the skewered tentacles. Grill them for 2 minutes on each side, until they start to scorch. Serve the stuffed squid with the tentacles. Add a few lemon wedges, for squeezing over the seafood.

Energy 357kcal/1496kJ; Protein 42.5g; Carbohydrate 3.5g, of which sugars 0.8g; Fat 19.4g, of which saturates 8.5g; Cholesterol 541mg; Calcium 209mg; Fibre 0g; Sodium 968mg.

ICED OYSTERS WITH MERGUEZ SAUSAGES

ALTHOUGH IT SEEMS AN UNUSUAL BARBECUE RECIPE, THESE TWO COMPLEMENT EACH OTHER PERFECTLY. MUNCH ON A LITTLE CHILLI-SPICED SAUSAGE, THEN QUELL THE BURNING SENSATION WITH THE CLEAN, COOL TEXTURE OF AN ICE-COLD OYSTER.

SERVES SIX

INGREDIENTS
675g/1½lb merguez sausages
crushed ice for serving
24 oysters
2 lemons, cut into wedges

1 Prepare the barbecue. Position a lightly oiled grill rack over the coals to heat. Place the sausages on the grill rack over medium-high heat. Grill them for 8 minutes, or until cooked through and golden, turning often.

2 Meanwhile, spread out the crushed ice on a platter and keep it chilled while you prepare the oysters. Scrub the oyster shells with a stiff brush to remove any sand. Make sure all the oysters are tightly closed, and discard any that aren't.

3 Place them on the grill rack, a few at a time, with the deep-side down, so that as they open the juices will be retained in the lower shell. They will begin to ease open after 3–5 minutes and must be removed from the heat immediately, so that they don't start to cook.

4 Lay the oysters on the ice. When they have all eased open, get to work with a sharp knife, opening them fully if need be. Remove the oysters from the flat side of the shell and place them with the juices on the deep half shells. Discard any oysters that fail to open. Serve with the hot, cooked sausages, and lemon wedges for squeezing.

Energy 439kcal/1820kJ; Protein 16.3g; Carbohydrate 11.8g, of which sugars 1.6g; Fat 36.6g, of which saturates 13.8g; Cholesterol 76mg; Calcium 102mg; Fibre 0.6g; Sodium 1059mg.

SIZZLING CHILLI SCALLOPS

SCALLOPS HAVE A BEAUTIFUL RICH FLAVOUR AND TASTE WONDERFUL BARBECUED WITH A SUBTLE CHILLI AND HONEY GLAZE. IF YOU ARE ABLE TO BUY QUEEN SCALLOPS IN THE HALF-SHELL THEY WILL BE READY TO GO ON THE BARBECUE - NOTHING COULD BE SIMPLER FOR A QUICK AND EXCEPTIONALLY TASTY DISH.

SERVES FOUR TO SIX

INGREDIENTS
    1 fresh fat mild green chilli, seeded
      and finely chopped
    ½–1 fresh Scotch bonnet or
      habañero chilli, seeded and
      finely chopped
    1 small shallot, finely chopped
    15ml/1 tbsp clear honey
    60ml/4 tbsp olive oil
    24 queen scallops on the half shell
    2 lemons, cut into thin wedges
    salt and ground black pepper

1 Prepare the barbecue. While it is heating, mix the chillies, shallot, honey and oil in a bowl.

2 Set out the scallops on a tray. Sprinkle each one with a pinch of salt, then top with a little of the chilli mixture. Position a grill rack over the coals to heat. Place the scallops, on their half shells, on the grill rack over medium-high heat.

3 Cook the scallops for 1½–2 minutes only. If your barbecue has enough space, cook as many as possible at once, moving them from the edge to the centre of the grill rack as necessary. Take care not to overcook them, or they will toughen. Place them on a serving platter, with the lemon wedges for squeezing. Serve immediately.

Energy 133kcal/554kJ; Protein 11.7g; Carbohydrate 3.6g, of which sugars 1.9g; Fat 8g, of which saturates 1.3g; Cholesterol 24mg; Calcium 15mg; Fibre 0g; Sodium 90mg.

CHARGRILLED TUNA SLICES

USE SASHIMI-QUALITY TUNA FROM A JAPANESE FOOD STORE OR FIRST-RATE FISHMONGER, WHO WILL TRIM IT TO A NEAT RECTANGULAR SHAPE. SERVE WITH JAPANESE SHISO LEAVES, OR SWEET BASIL.

SERVES FOUR

INGREDIENTS

15g/½oz dried arame seaweed,
  soaked in water
60ml/4 tbsp tamari
30ml/2 tbsp mirin
120ml/4fl oz/½ cup water
5ml/1 tsp white sesame seeds
15ml/1 tbsp black sesame seeds
10ml/2 tsp dried pink peppercorns
2.5ml/½ tsp sunflower oil
250g/9oz sashimi tuna
16 fresh shiso leaves
7.5ml/1½ tsp wasabi paste
50g/2oz mooli (daikon),
  finely grated

1 Drain the arame, then soak it in a bowl with the tamari, mirin and water for 1 hour. Pour the liquid from the arame into a small pan and put the arame in a serving bowl.

2 Bring the liquid to a simmer. Cook for 3–5 minutes, or until syrupy, cool for 2 minutes and pour over the arame. Scatter with the white sesame seeds and cover until needed.

3 Prepare the barbecue. Lightly grind the black sesame seeds and pink peppercorns in a spice mill. Brush the oil over the tuna, then roll the tuna into the spice mixture to coat it evenly.

4 Heat a griddle on a grill rack over hot coals. Sear the tuna for 30 seconds on each of the four sides. Using a very sharp knife, slice it into 5mm/¼in wide pieces and arrange on plates with the shiso leaves, a blob of wasabi and a mound each of arame and grated mooli.

CHICKEN SATAY STICKS

PANDANUS LEAVES ARE COMMON TO THAI AND SOUTH-EAST ASIAN COOKING, AND ARE SOMETIMES ALSO KNOWN AS SCREWPINE OR BANDAN LEAVES. THEY ARE ENORMOUSLY VERSATILE, AND ARE USED HERE FOR THE DELICATE FLAVOUR THEY BRING TO THE CHICKEN, AS WELL AS THEIR VISUAL APPEAL.

SERVES SIX

INGREDIENTS

about 1kg/2¼lb skinless chicken
   breast fillets
30ml/2 tbsp olive oil
5ml/1 tsp ground coriander
2.5ml/½ tsp ground cumin
2.5cm/1in piece of fresh root ginger,
   finely grated
2 garlic cloves, crushed
5ml/1 tsp caster (superfine) sugar
2.5ml/½ tsp salt
18 long pandanus leaves, each
   halved to give 21cm/8½in lengths
For the hot cashew nut sambal
2 garlic cloves, roughly chopped
4 small fresh hot green chillies (not
   tiny birdseye chillies), seeded and
   sliced
50g/2oz/⅓ cup cashew nuts
10ml/2 tsp sugar, preferably
   palm sugar
75ml/5 tbsp light soy sauce
juice of ½ lime
30ml/2 tbsp coconut cream

1 To make the sambal, place the garlic and chillies in a mortar and grind them quite finely with a pestle. Add the nuts and continue to grind until the mixture is almost smooth, with just a bit of texture. Pound in the remaining ingredients, cover and put in a cool place until needed.

2 Soak 36 long bamboo or wooden skewers in water for 30 minutes. Slice the chicken horizontally into thin pieces and then into strips about 2.5cm/1in wide. Toss in the oil. Mix the coriander, cumin, ginger, garlic, sugar and salt together. Rub this mixture into the strips of chicken. Leave to marinate while you prepare the barbecue.

3 Thread a strip of pandanus leaf and a piece of chicken lengthways on to each skewer. Once the flames have died down, rake the coals to one side. Position a lightly oiled grill rack over the coals to heat.

4 Place the satays meat-side down over the coals and cover with a lid or some tented heavy-duty foil and cook for 5–7 minutes. Once the meat has seared, move the satays around so that they are not cooking directly over the coals. This will avoid the leaves becoming scorched. Serve hot with the sambal.

COOK'S TIP
The easiest way to make the sambal is to use a deep Thai mortar. The resulting mixture will have a satisfying crunch rather than being a smooth purée.

Energy 280kcal/1178kJ; Protein 42.3g; Carbohydrate 5.9g, of which sugars 4.6g; Fat 9.8g, of which saturates 1.9g; Cholesterol 117mg; Calcium 19mg; Fibre 0.5g; Sodium 1026mg.

PORK ᴼᴺ LEMON GRASS STICKS

THIS SIMPLE RECIPE MAKES A SUBSTANTIAL APPETIZER, AND THE LEMON GRASS STICKS NOT ONLY ADD A SUBTLE FLAVOUR BUT ALSO LOOK MOST ATTRACTIVE.

SERVES FOUR

INGREDIENTS
   300g/11oz minced (ground) pork
   4 garlic cloves, crushed
   4 fresh coriander (cilantro) roots,
      finely chopped
   2.5ml/½ tsp granulated sugar
   15ml/1 tbsp soy sauce
   8 x 10cm/4in lengths of lemon
      grass stalk
   salt and ground black pepper
   sweet chilli sauce,
      to serve

VARIATION
Slimmer versions of these pork sticks are perfect for parties. The mixture will be enough for 12 lemon grass sticks if you use it sparingly.

1 Place the minced pork, crushed garlic, chopped coriander root, sugar and soy sauce in a large bowl. Season with salt and pepper to taste, and mix well.

2 Divide into eight portions and mould each one into a ball. It may help to dampen your hands before shaping the mixture to prevent it from sticking.

3 Stick a length of lemon grass halfway into each ball, then press the meat mixture around it.

4 Prepare the barbecue. Position a lightly oiled grill rack over the hot coals. Cook the pork sticks for 3–4 minutes on each side, until golden and cooked through. Serve with the chilli sauce for dipping.

Energy 97kcal/409kJ; Protein 16.6g; Carbohydrate 0.7g, of which sugars 0.6g; Fat 3.2g, of which saturates 1.1g; Cholesterol 47mg; Calcium 31mg; Fibre 0.6g; Sodium 324mg.

MINI BURGERS WITH MOZZARELLA

THESE ITALIAN-STYLE PATTIES ARE MADE WITH BEEF AND TOPPED WITH CREAMY MELTED MOZZARELLA AND SAVOURY ANCHOVIES. THEY MAKE A SUBSTANTIAL AND UNUSUAL APPETIZER.

SERVES SIX

INGREDIENTS
½ slice white bread, crusts removed
45ml/3 tbsp milk
675g/1½lb minced (ground) beef
1 egg, beaten
50g/2oz/⅔ cup dry breadcrumbs
olive oil, for brushing
2 beefsteak or other large tomatoes, sliced
15ml/1 tbsp chopped fresh oregano
1 mozzarella, cut into 6 slices
6 drained, canned anchovy fillets, cut in half lengthways
salt and ground black pepper

1 Put the bread and milk into a small pan and heat gently, until the bread absorbs all the milk. Mash and leave to cool.

2 Put the minced beef into a bowl and add the cooled bread mixture. Stir in the beaten egg and season with plenty of salt and freshly ground black pepper. Mix well.

3 Shape the mixture into six patties, using your hands. Sprinkle the dry breadcrumbs on to a plate and dredge the patties, coating them thoroughly all over.

4 Prepare the barbecue. Position a lightly oiled grill rack over the hot coals. Brush the patties with olive oil and cook them on a hot barbecue for 2–3 minutes on one side, or until brown. Turn them over.

5 Without removing the patties from the barbecue, lay a slice of tomato on top of each patty, sprinkle with chopped oregano and season with salt and pepper. Place a mozzarella slice on top and arrange two strips of anchovy in a cross over the cheese.

6 Cook for a further 4–5 minutes, or until the patties are cooked through and the mozzarella has melted.

Energy 360kcal/1499kJ; Protein 28.6g; Carbohydrate 9.6g, of which sugars 2.2g; Fat 23.2g, of which saturates 10.9g; Cholesterol 82mg; Calcium 121mg; Fibre 0.7g; Sodium 374mg.

FISH AND SHELLFISH

Fresh seafood tastes great when it is barbecued, and there are so many ways that fish and shellfish can be prepared. Wrap them in leaves or steam inside foil parcels, cut them into chunks and skewer, stuff them or simply brush with oil or a fresh marinade and cook straight on the barbecue. Some of the fastest foods to cook over coals are shellfish, so they are perfect for that impromptu meal. Small whole fish are also an ideal choice for a quick bite to eat, but if you have a little more time, try some of the rewarding recipes that include sauces or relishes, or those dishes that require marinating a little way in advance; these simple touches and techniques will transform barbecued seafood — and the cooking aromas, with their promise of flavour, will tempt the tastebuds of any party guest. If you are planning to eat on the beach, there is even a Seafood Bake where you can cook locally caught shellfish without using a conventional barbecue.

SEAFOOD on SUGAR CANE

TOLEE MOLEE IS A BURMESE TERM FOR THE BITS AND PIECES THAT GO WITH A MAIN COURSE, SUCH AS BOWLS OF HERBS, CRISPY FRIED ONIONS AND BALACHAUNG, A CHILLI AND PRAWN PASTE. IF YOU PREFER, SPIKE THE PRAWNS ON SKEWERS RATHER THAN SUGAR CANE.

MAKES TWELVE

INGREDIENTS
400g/14oz king prawns (jumbo
    shrimp), peeled
225g/8oz skinned cod or halibut
    fillet, roughly cut into pieces
pinch of ground turmeric
1.5ml/¼ tsp ground white pepper
1.5ml/¼ tsp salt
60ml/4 tbsp chopped fresh coriander
    (cilantro)
1 fresh long red chilli, seeded and
    finely chopped
a piece of sugar cane cut into
    12 spikes (see Cook's Tip)
    or 12 wooden skewers
30ml/2 tbsp sunflower oil
For the tolee molee
25g/1oz/1 cup coriander
    (cilantro) leaves
45ml/3 tbsp olive oil
300g/11oz sweet onions, halved and
    finely sliced
90ml/6 tbsp balachaung
15ml/1 tbsp sugar
juice of ½ lime
30ml/2 tbsp water

1 Soak the sugar cane spikes or skewers in water for 30 minutes. Make a shallow cut down the centre of the curved back of the prawns. Pull out the black veins with a cocktail stick (toothpick). Slice the prawns roughly and place in a food processor with the fish, turmeric, pepper and salt.

2 Pulse until the mixture forms a paste. Add the coriander and chilli, and pulse lightly to combine with the other ingredients. Spoon into a bowl and chill for 30 minutes.

3 To make the tolee molee, place the coriander leaves in a small serving bowl filled with cold water. Chill. Heat the olive oil in a large frying pan and fry the sliced onions over a medium heat for 10 minutes, stirring occasionally and increasing the heat for the last few minutes so that the onions become golden and crisp.

4 Pile the cooked onions into a serving bowl. Place the balachaung in another serving bowl, and mix in the sugar, lime juice and measured water. Stir the mixture thoroughly and set aside.

5 Using damp hands, mould the seafood mixture around the drained sugarcane spikes or wooden skewers, so that it forms an oval sausage shape.

6 Prepare the barbecue. Position a lightly oiled grill rack over the hot coals. Brush the seafood with the sunflower oil and grill over medium-high heat for about 3 minutes on each side until just cooked through. Serve with the tolee molee.

COOK'S TIP
To make sugar cane spikes, chop through the length using a cook's knife and split into 1cm/½in shards. The sugar cane can be bought from ethnic grocers.

Energy 98kcal/410kJ; Protein 9.9g; Carbohydrate 3.5g, of which sugars 2.9g; Fat 5.1g, of which saturates 0.7g; Cholesterol 74mg; Calcium 52mg; Fibre 0.8g; Sodium 78mg.

MARINATED OCTOPUS ON STICKS

OCTOPUS THAT IS FROZEN AND THEN THAWED BECOMES TENDER IN THE PROCESS, AND SO IT COOKS QUICKLY. CHECK WITH THE FISHMONGER BEFORE BUYING, BECAUSE FRESH OCTOPUS WILL NEED CONSIDERABLY MORE SIMMERING TIME. SERVE WITH RED PIPIAN FOR A SPICY PUNCH.

SERVES EIGHT

INGREDIENTS
1kg/2¼lb whole octopus
1 onion, quartered
2 bay leaves
30ml/2 tbsp olive oil
grated rind and juice of 1 lemon
15ml/1 tbsp chopped fresh coriander
  (cilantro)
For the red pipian
  1 ancho chilli (dried poblano)
  4 whole garlic cloves, peeled
  1 small pink onion, chopped
  500g/1¼lb plum tomatoes, cored
    and seeded
  30ml/2 tbsp olive oil
  5ml/1 tsp sugar
  30ml/2 tbsp pine nuts
  30ml/2 tbsp pumpkin seeds
  pinch of ground cinnamon
  15ml/1 tbsp chipotles in adobo
    or other sweet and smoky chilli
    sauce
  45ml/3 tbsp vegetable stock
  leaves from 4 large fresh thyme
    sprigs, finely chopped
  salt
  fresh coriander (cilantro) sprigs,
    to garnish

1 Make the red pipian. Preheat the oven to 200°C/400°F/Gas 6. Put the ancho chilli in a bowl and cover with hot water. Leave to soak for about 20 minutes. Meanwhile place the garlic, onion and tomatoes in a roasting pan and drizzle with the oil, then sprinkle the sugar and a little salt over the top. Roast for 15 minutes. Add the pine nuts, pumpkin seeds and cinnamon to the top of the mixture and roast for a further 5 minutes. Meanwhile, drain the ancho chilli, remove the seeds and chop the flesh.

2 Transfer the roasted mixture and the ancho chilli to a food processor with the chipotles or chilli sauce, vegetable stock and thyme. Pulse to a purée, then scrape into a serving bowl and leave to cool.

COOK'S TIP
Cook the skewered octopus on a griddle, if you prefer. The timing will be the same.

3 Trim the tentacles from the head of the octopus. Leave the skin on, but trim any large flaps with kitchen scissors. Discard the head. Place the tentacles in a large pan, cover with cold water and add the onion and bay leaves. Bring slowly to the boil, lower the heat and simmer for about 20 minutes if pre-frozen, and up to 2 hours if fresh.

4 Drain the tentacles and rinse under cold water, rubbing off any loose dark membrane. Thread the tentacles on to eight metal skewers and put in a plastic bag with the olive oil, lemon rind and juice, and chopped coriander. Tie shut and shake to mix. Leave to marinate in a cool place for at least 1 hour or up to 12 hours.

5 Prepare the barbecue. Position a lightly oiled grill rack over the hot coals. Grill the octopus skewers over medium-high heat for 2–4 minutes each side, or until nicely golden. Serve with the red pipian, garnished with the coriander sprigs.

Energy 149kcal/627kJ; Protein 23.2g; Carbohydrate 3.8g, of which sugars 3.4g; Fat 4.7g, of which saturates 0.8g; Cholesterol 60mg; Calcium 62mg; Fibre 1.2g; Sodium 8mg.

SEAFOOD AND SPRING ONION SKEWERS

MONKFISH IS A FINE FISH FOR BARBECUING, AS ITS FIRM FLESH HOLDS ITS SHAPE WELL AND IS EASY TO SPEAR ON TO SKEWERS. IT HAS A LOVELY SWEET FLAVOUR, VERY SIMILAR TO SHELLFISH, AND HERE IT IS PARTNERED WITH SCALLOPS OR KING PRAWNS, MAKING AN ATTRACTIVE AND DELICIOUS COMBINATION.

MAKES NINE

INGREDIENTS

   675g/1½lb monkfish, filleted,
     skinned and membrane removed
   1 bunch thick spring onions
     (scallions), cut into 5cm/2in pieces
   75ml/5 tbsp olive oil
   1 garlic clove, finely chopped
   15ml/1 tbsp lemon juice
   5ml/1 tsp dried oregano
   30ml/2 tbsp chopped fresh flat
     leaf parsley
   12–18 small scallops or raw king
     prawns (jumbo shrimp)
   75g/3oz/1½ cups fine fresh
     breadcrumbs
   salt and ground black pepper
For the tartare sauce
   2 egg yolks
   300ml/½ pint/1¼ cups olive oil,
     or vegetable oil and olive oil mixed
   15–30ml/1–2 tbsp lemon juice
   5ml/1 tsp French mustard, preferably
     tarragon mustard
   15ml/1 tbsp chopped gherkin or
     pickled cucumber
   15ml/1 tbsp chopped capers
   30ml/2 tbsp chopped fresh flat
     leaf parsley
   30ml/2 tbsp chopped fresh chives
   5ml/1 tsp chopped fresh tarragon

1 Soak nine wooden skewers in water for 30 minutes to prevent them from scorching on the barbecue.

2 To make the tartare sauce, whisk the egg yolks and a pinch of salt. Whisk in the oil, a drop at a time at first. When about half the oil is incorporated, add it in a thin stream, whisking constantly. Stop when the mayonnaise is thick.

3 Whisk in 15ml/1 tbsp lemon juice, then a little more oil. Stir in the mustard, gherkin or cucumber, capers, parsley, chives and tarragon. Add more lemon juice and seasoning to taste.

4 Cut the monkfish into 18 pieces. In a bowl, mix the oil, garlic, lemon juice, oregano and half the parsley with seasoning. Add the seafood and spring onions. Leave to marinate for 15 minutes.

5 Mix the breadcrumbs and remaining parsley together. Toss the seafood and spring onions in the mixture to coat.

6 Prepare the barbecue. Position a lightly oiled grill rack over the hot coals. Drain the wooden skewers and thread the monkfish, scallops or prawns and spring onions on to them. Drizzle with a little marinade then cook over medium heat for 7–8 minutes in total, turning once and drizzling with the marinade, until the fish is just cooked. Serve immediately with the tartare sauce.

Energy 352kcal/1462kJ; Protein 16.6g; Carbohydrate 6.9g, of which sugars 0.6g; Fat 28.9g, of which saturates 4.3g; Cholesterol 88mg; Calcium 41mg; Fibre 0.4g; Sodium 111mg.

GRILLED LOBSTER

THIS IS A SMART YET UNPRETENTIOUS DISH AND WELL WORTH THE LITTLE BIT OF EXTRA EFFORT. LOBSTER IS A FANTASTIC INGREDIENT TO COOK WITH BUT, IF YOU ARE A BIT SQUEAMISH, DISPATCHING IT IS A VERY HARD THING TO DO, IN WHICH CASE IT IS A JOB PROBABLY BEST LEFT TO THE FISHMONGER. INSTRUCTIONS FOR KILLING IT HUMANELY ARE GIVEN BELOW.

SERVES TWO TO FOUR

INGREDIENTS
    15 fresh basil leaves, roughly
       chopped
    60ml/4 tbsp olive oil
    1 garlic clove, crushed
    2 freshly killed lobsters, cut in
       half lengthways and cleaned
       (see Cook's Tip)
    salt and ground black pepper
    2 limes, halved, to serve
For the basil oil and mayonnaise
    40g/1½oz/1½ cups basil leaves
       stripped from their stalks
    175ml/6fl oz/¾ cup sunflower oil,
       plus extra if needed
    45ml/3 tbsp olive oil
    1 small garlic clove, crushed
    2.5ml/½ tsp dry English (hot)
       mustard
    10ml/2 tsp lemon juice
    2 egg yolks
    ground white pepper

1 To make the basil oil, place the basil leaves in a bowl and pour boiling water over them. Leave for about 30 seconds until the leaves turn a brighter green. Drain, refresh under cold running water, drain again, then squeeze dry in kitchen paper. Place the leaves in a food processor. Add both oils and process to a purée. Scrape into a bowl, cover and chill overnight.

2 Line a sieve with muslin and set it over a deep bowl. Pour in the basil and oil purée and leave undisturbed for about 1 hour, or until all the oil has filtered through into the bowl. Discard the solids left behind. Cover and chill.

3 To make the mayonnaise, you will need 200ml/7fl oz/ scant 1 cup of the basil oil. If you do not have enough, make it up with more sunflower oil. Place the crushed garlic in a bowl. Add the mustard with 2.5ml/ ½ tsp of the lemon juice and a little salt and white pepper.

4 Whisk in the egg yolks, then start adding the basil oil, a drop at a time, whisking continuously until the mixture starts to thicken. At this stage it is usually safe to start adding the oil a little faster. When you have 45ml/3 tbsp oil left, whisk in the remaining lemon juice and then add the rest of the oil. Finally, whisk in 7.5ml/1½ tsp cold water. Cover the mayonnaise and chill.

5 Prepare the barbecue. Chop the basil and mix it with the oil and garlic in a bowl. Season lightly. Once the flames have died down, rake the coals to get more on one side than the other. Position a lightly oiled grill rack over the coals to heat.

6 Brush some of the oil mixture over the cut side of each lobster half. Place cut-side down on the grill rack on the side away from the bulk of the coals. Grill for 5 minutes. Turn the lobsters over, baste with more oil mixture and cook for 10–15 minutes more, basting and moving them about the rack.

7 Grill the lime halves at the same time, placing them cut-side down for 3 minutes to caramelize. Serve the lobster with the mayonnaise and the grilled lime halves.

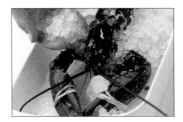

COOK'S TIP
If you have to kill a lobster yourself, you can do so humanely. Either put the live lobster in a freezerproof dish or tray and cover with crushed ice to render it unconscious, or put it into the freezer for 2 hours. When the lobster is very cold and no longer moving, place it on a chopping board and drive the tip of a large, sharp and heavy knife or a very strong skewer through the centre of the cross on its head. According to experts, death is instantaneous.

To clean, split in half by laying the lobster on its back and stretching out the body. Use a sharp, heavy knife to cut the lobster neatly in half along the entire length. Discard the whitish sac and the feathery gills from the head and the grey-black intestinal sac that runs down the tail. The greenish tomalley (liver) and the coral (roe) are delicious, so retain these.

Energy 518kcal/2144kJ; Protein 21.8g; Carbohydrate 0.4g, of which sugars 0.3g; Fat 47.9g, of which saturates 6.5g; Cholesterol 201mg; Calcium 92mg; Fibre 0.6g; Sodium 309mg.

TIGER PRAWN SKEWERS

LARGE PRAWNS ARE FULL OF FLAVOUR AND IDEAL FOR BARBECUING — AND THEY ARE SO QUICK TO COOK. IN THIS RECIPE THEY ARE MARINATED IN AN UNUSUAL WALNUT PESTO, WHICH IS SIMPLE TO PREPARE AND CAN BE MADE THE DAY BEFORE. MARINATE OVERNIGHT FOR THE BEST RESULTS.

SERVES FOUR

INGREDIENTS

12–16 large, raw, shell-on tiger
   prawns (jumbo shrimp)
50g/2oz/½ cup walnut pieces
60ml/4 tbsp chopped fresh flat
   leaf parsley
60ml/4 tbsp chopped fresh basil
2 garlic cloves, chopped
45ml/3 tbsp grated fresh
   Parmesan cheese
30ml/2 tbsp extra virgin olive oil
30ml/2 tbsp walnut oil
salt and ground black pepper

1 Peel the prawns, removing the head but leaving the tail. Devein the prawns using a cocktail stick (toothpick) and then put the prawns in a large mixing bowl.

VARIATION
For garlic prawns, clean the prawns and thread on skewers. Brush with oil and grill as before. Melt 50g/2oz/¼ cup butter in a small pan on the barbecue. Add 2 crushed garlic cloves, 30ml/2 tbsp chopped fresh parsley, the grated rind of ¼ lemon and 15ml/1 tbsp lemon juice. Serve with the prawns.

2 To make the pesto, place the walnuts, parsley, basil, garlic, cheese and oils in a food processor and process until finely chopped. Season.

3 Add half the pesto to the prawns in the bowl, toss them well, then cover and chill for a minimum of 1 hour, or leave them overnight.

4 Soak four wooden skewers in water for 30 minutes. Prepare the barbecue. Position a lightly oiled grill rack over the hot coals. Thread the prawns on to the skewers and cook them over high heat for 3–4 minutes, turning once. Serve with the remaining pesto and a green salad, if you like.

Energy 256kcal/1062kJ; Protein 13.9g; Carbohydrate 0.9g, of which sugars 0.8g; Fat 21.9g, of which saturates 4.2g; Cholesterol 90mg; Calcium 209mg; Fibre 1.3g; Sodium 578mg.

MARINATED MONKFISH AND MUSSEL KEBABS

*THIS RECIPE COMBINES SEAFOOD WITH TURKEY, GIVING THE KEBABS EXTRA RICHNESS. THE SIMPLE
MARINADE TAKES NO TIME AT ALL TO PREPARE. THE MARINADE WILL MAKE THE MONKFISH BOTH
DELICIOUSLY FLAVOURED AND QUICKER TO BARBECUE, SO OBSERVE THE COOKING TIME CLOSELY.*

SERVES FOUR

INGREDIENTS
    450g/1lb monkfish, skinned
      and boned
    5ml/1 tsp olive oil
    30ml/2 tbsp lemon juice
    5ml/1 tsp paprika
    1 garlic clove, crushed
    4 turkey rashers
    8 cooked mussels
    8 large raw prawns (shrimp)
    15ml/1 tbsp chopped fresh dill
    salt and ground black pepper
    lemon wedges, to garnish
    salad and rice, to serve

1 Mix together the oil, lemon juice,
paprika, and garlic in a bowl and
season with pepper.

2 Cut the monkfish into 2.5cm/1in
cubes and place in a shallow glass dish.

3 Pour the marinade over the fish and
toss to coat evenly. Cover and leave in a
cool place for 30 minutes.

4 Cut the turkey rashers in half and
wrap each strip around a mussel.
Thread on to skewers alternating with
the fish cubes and raw prawns.

COOK'S TIP
If you thread your kebabs on to two
parallel skewers you will find they are
easier to turn over.

5 Prepare the barbecue. Position a
lightly oiled grill rack over the hot coals.
Cook the kebabs over high heat for
7–8 minutes, turning once and basting
with the marinade. Sprinkle with
chopped dill and salt. Garnish with the
lemon wedges and serve with salad
and rice.

Energy 126kcal/534kJ; Protein 26.5g; Carbohydrate 0.3g, of which sugars 0g; Fat 2.1g, of which saturates 0.5g; Cholesterol 67mg; Calcium 26mg; Fibre 0g; Sodium 103mg.

SEAFOOD BAKE

A BEACH BAKE IS GREAT FUN AND A SEMI-PRECISE SCIENCE, WHICH REQUIRES COMMITMENT BY AT LEAST TWO HIGHLY MOTIVATED PARTIES WITH A PENCHANT FOR DIGGING HOLES. BASE YOUR CATCH ON THE INGREDIENTS BELOW, MULTIPLIED AS REQUIRED.

SERVES ONE

INGREDIENTS
  2 freshwater crayfish
  4 langoustines
  2 large clams, about 6cm/2½in
    across
  6 small clams
  3 whelks
  12 cockles
  lemons, bread and good quality
    olive oil
Other things you will need
  sand or earth
  shovels and buckets
  dry pebbles
  plenty of dry firewood, newspaper
    and twigs
  matches or a lighter
  long-handled rake
  seaweed, well washed and soaked
    in water
  a large piece of canvas, soaked
    in water
  12 heavy stones
  heatproof gloves
  cocktail sticks (toothpicks)

1 Dig a pit at least 90cm/3ft square x 30cm/1ft deep; larger if you are catering for a crowd. Line the base with pebbles, taking them part of the way up the sides. Build a pyramid-shaped mound of kindling in the middle of the square, with some scrunched-up newspaper at the base.

2 Start the fire. When the wood is burning well, add larger pieces to the fire so that it eventually covers the entire surface area of the pit. Keep the fire well stoked up for about 45–60 minutes, then let it burn down to a stage where small glowing embers remain. Using a long-handled rake, pull as many of the dying embers as possible from the pit without dislodging the pebbles.

3 At this point it is important to retain the oven-like temperature of the pebbles so, working quickly, spread half the seaweed evenly over the pebbles. Arrange the seafood over the seaweed, with the smallest items towards the edges for easy access, as these will cook first. Cover with the rest of the seaweed, then cover the lot with the wet canvas. This should extend beyond the perimeter of the pit and should be weighted down with 12 heavy stones, placed well away from the pit.

4 Leave the seafood to bake undisturbed for 1–2 hours. The hotter the pebbles get, the faster the food will cook, so after 1 hour, have a sneaky peek to see if the cockles and small clams are cooked. These can be taken out at this stage and eaten, and the rest of the seafood enjoyed when it is ready.

COOK'S TIP
Before leaving the site, take care to douse any discarded embers with water to ensure they are not left hot.

Energy 175kcal/742kJ; Protein 38.9g; Carbohydrate 0.9g, of which sugars 0g; Fat 1.8g, of which saturates 0.4g; Cholesterol 268mg; Calcium 164mg; Fibre 0g; Sodium 1139mg.

SCALLOPS WITH LIME BUTTER

CHARGRILLING FENNEL RELEASES ITS ANISEED FLAVOUR, WHICH TASTES GREAT WITH SWEET AND RICH SCALLOPS. THESE WONDERFUL SHELLFISH ARE IDEAL FOR THE BARBECUE BECAUSE THEY HAVE FIRM FLESH THAT COOKS QUICKLY — SIMPLY TOSS IN LIME JUICE BEFORE COOKING.

SERVES FOUR

INGREDIENTS
1 head fennel
2 limes
12 large scallops, cleaned
1 egg yolk
90ml/6 tbsp melted butter
olive oil for brushing
salt and ground black pepper

COOK'S TIP
When choosing fennel, look for bulbs that are white and firm.

1 Trim any feathery leaves from the fennel and reserve them. Slice the rest lengthways into thin wedges.

2 Cut one lime into wedges. Finely grate the rind and squeeze the juice of the other lime and toss half the juice and rind on to the scallops. Season well with salt and ground black pepper.

3 Place the egg yolk and remaining lime rind and juice in a small bowl and whisk until pale and smooth.

4 Gradually whisk in the melted butter and continue whisking until thick and smooth. Finely chop the reserved fennel leaves and stir them in, with seasoning.

5 Prepare the barbecue. Position a lightly oiled grill rack over the hot coals. Brush the fennel wedges with olive oil and cook them over high heat for 3–4 minutes, turning once.

6 Add the scallops and cook for a further 3–4 minutes, turning once. Serve with the lime and fennel butter and the lime wedges.

COOK'S TIP
Thread small scallops on to flat skewers to make turning them easier.

Energy 232kcal/961kJ; Protein 10g; Carbohydrate 2.2g, of which sugars 0.9g; Fat 20.5g, of which saturates 12.3g; Cholesterol 116mg; Calcium 31mg; Fibre 1.1g; Sodium 211mg.

ROLLED SARDINES <u>WITH</u> PLUM PASTE

MAKE THIS SIMPLE AND DELIGHTFUL JAPANESE RECIPE WHEN SARDINES ARE IN SEASON. PERFECTLY
FRESH SARDINES ARE ROLLED UP AROUND LAYERS OF SHISO LEAVES AND UMEBOSHI, A JAPANESE
APRICOT (OFTEN CALLED 'JAPANESE PLUM') THAT IS PICKLED IN SALT.

SERVES FOUR

INGREDIENTS
    8 sardines, cleaned and filleted
    5ml/1 tsp salt
    4 umeboshi, about 30g/1¼oz total
        weight (choose the soft type)
    5ml/1 tsp sake
    5ml/1 tsp toasted sesame seeds
    16 shiso leaves, cut in
        half lengthways
    1 lime, thinly sliced, the centre
        hollowed out to make rings,
        to garnish

COOK'S TIP
Sardines deteriorate very quickly and
must be bought and eaten on the same
day. Be careful when buying: the eyes
and gills should not be too pink. If the
fish "melts" like cheese when grilled,
don't bother to eat it.

1 Carefully cut the sardine fillets in half
lengthways and place them side by side
in a large, shallow container. Sprinkle
with salt on both sides.

2 Remove the stones (pits) from the
umeboshi and put the fruit in a small
mixing bowl with the sake and toasted
sesame seeds. With the back of a fork,
mash the umeboshi, mixing well to form
a smooth paste.

3 Wipe the sardine fillets with kitchen
paper. With a butter knife, spread some
umeboshi paste thinly on to one of the
sardine fillets, then press some shiso
leaves on top. Roll up the sardine
starting from the tail and pierce with a
wooden cocktail stick (toothpick).
Repeat to make 16 rolled sardines.

4 Prepare the barbecue. Position a
lightly oiled grill rack over the hot coals.
Grill the rolled sardines over medium-
high heat for 4–6 minutes on each side,
or until golden brown, turning once.

5 Lay a few lime rings on four individual
plates and arrange the rolled sardines
alongside. Serve hot.

Energy 248kcal/1037kJ; Protein 31.1g; Carbohydrate 0.7g, of which sugars 0.7g; Fat 13.3g, of which saturates 3.7g; Cholesterol 0mg; Calcium 161mg; Fibre 0.2g; Sodium 171mg.

SALMON KEBABS WITH COCONUT

KEBABS MAKE EXCITING BARBECUE FOOD, BECAUSE YOU CAN COOK A VARIETY OF FLAVOURS TOGETHER WITHOUT LOSING THEIR INDIVIDUAL IDENTITIES. INSPIRED BY FLAVOURS FROM THE WEST INDIES, THIS RECIPE COMBINES COCONUT AND LIME TO COMPLEMENT THE SUBTLE TASTE OF THE SEAFOOD.

3 Cut each lime into six slices. Thread the coconut, salmon, scallops and pieces of lime alternately on to the skewers.

4 Add the lime juice, soy sauce, honey and sugar to the coconut liquor to make the marinade. Season with pepper.

5 Place the prepared kebabs in a single layer in a shallow non-metallic dish. Pour the marinade over. Cover and chill for at least 3 hours.

SERVES SIX

INGREDIENTS
  450g/1lb salmon fillet, skinned
  1 small fresh coconut
  2 limes
  12 scallops
  45ml/3 tbsp freshly squeezed
    lime juice
  30ml/2 tbsp soy sauce
  30ml/2 tbsp clear honey
  15ml/1 tbsp soft light brown sugar
  ground black pepper

COOK'S TIP
The best way to open a coconut is to hold it in the palm of your hand, with the "eyes" just above your thumb. The fault line lies between the eyes. Hold over a bowl to catch the liquid, then carefully hit the line with the blunt side of a cleaver or hammer so that it splits into two halves.

1 Soak six wooden skewers in water for 30 minutes. Using a sharp knife, cut the salmon into bite size chunks and place these in a shallow bowl.

2 Halve the coconut as instructed (see cook's tip) and pour the liquor into a jug (pitcher). Using a small, sharp knife, remove the coconut flesh from the inside of the shell and cut into chunks, about the same size as the salmon.

6 Preheat the barbecue. Position a lightly oiled grill rack over the hot coals. Transfer the kebabs to the barbecue and cook for 4 minutes on each side, basting with the marinade.

Energy 265kcal/1102kJ; Protein 20.8g; Carbohydrate 3.2g, of which sugars 2.5g; Fat 18.9g, of which saturates 10.4g; Cholesterol 47mg; Calcium 26mg; Fibre 2.3g; Sodium 193mg.

HERBY WRAPPED SALMON

THIS PARSI DISH, WITH ITS ORIGINS IN PERSIAN COOKING, USES A TOPPING FOR SALMON THAT IS BURSTING WITH THE FLAVOURS OF COCONUT, GARLIC, CHILLI, FRESH HERBS AND FENUGREEK. IT IS WRAPPED IN MOIST BANANA LEAVES TO SEAL IN THE FLAVOUR AND COOK THE FISH PERFECTLY.

SERVES SIX

INGREDIENTS

50g/2oz fresh coconut, skinned and finely grated, or 65g/2½oz/scant 1 cup desiccated (dry unsweetened shredded) coconut, soaked in 30ml/2 tbsp water
1 large lemon, skin, pith and seeds removed, roughly chopped
4 large garlic cloves, crushed
3 large fresh mild green chillies, seeded and chopped
50g/2oz/2 cups fresh coriander (cilantro), roughly chopped
25g/1oz/1 cup fresh mint leaves, roughly chopped
5ml/1 tsp ground cumin
5ml/1 tsp sugar
2.5ml/½ tsp fenugreek seeds, finely ground
5ml/1 tsp salt
2 large, whole banana leaves
6 salmon fillets, about 1.2kg/2½lb total weight, skinned

1 Place all the ingredients except the banana leaves and salmon in a food processor. Pulse to a fine paste. Scrape the mixture into a bowl, cover and chill for 30 minutes.

2 Prepare the barbecue. To make the parcels, cut each banana leaf widthways into three and cut off the hard outside edge from each piece. Put the pieces of leaf and the edge strips in a bowl of hot water. Leave for about 10 minutes. Drain, gently wipe off any white residue, rinse the leaves and strips, and pour over boiling water to soften. Drain, then place the leaves, smooth-side up, on a clean board.

3 Smear the top and bottom of each fillet with the coconut paste, then place one on each leaf. Bring the trimmed edge of the leaf over the salmon, then fold in the sides. Bring up the remaining edge to cover the salmon and make a neat parcel. Tie securely with a leaf strip.

4 Lay each parcel on a sheet of heavy-duty foil, bring up the edges and scrunch the tops together to seal. Position a lightly oiled grill rack over the hot coals. Place the salmon parcels on the grill rack and cook over medium-high heat for about 10 minutes, turning them over once.

5 Place the foil-wrapped parcels on individual plates and leave to stand for 2–3 minutes – the salmon will continue to cook for a while in the residual heat of the parcel. Remove the foil, then carefully unwrap so that the fish is resting on the opened leaves, then eat straight out of the banana leaf parcel.

COOK'S TIP
Serve little rice parcels with the fish. Fill six more banana leaf packages with cooked basmati rice coloured with ground turmeric, secure each one with a skewer and reheat on the barbecue.

Energy 430kcal/1789kJ; Protein 41.4g; Carbohydrate 1.1g, of which sugars 0.9g; Fat 28.9g, of which saturates 9.6g; Cholesterol 100mg; Calcium 70mg; Fibre 1.9g; Sodium 96mg.

FISH BROCHETTES WITH PEPERONATA

IN THIS DISH, THE PEPPERS FOR THE PEPERONATA ARE ROASTED AND SKINNED, GIVING IT A LOVELY SMOKY FLAVOUR AND SMOOTH TEXTURE, WHILE THE VERJUICE, AN UNFERMENTED GRAPE JUICE, ADDS AN UNDERLYING TARTNESS. IT IS EXCELLENT SERVED WITH FISH KEBABS.

SERVES FOUR

INGREDIENTS
 8 fresh sprigs of bay leaves
 675g/1½lb mahi-mahi, swordfish or
   marlin fillet, skinned
 1 lime, halved
 1 lemon, halved
 60ml/4 tbsp olive oil
 1 small garlic clove, crushed
 salt and ground black pepper
For the peperonata
 2 large red (bell) peppers, quartered
   and seeded
 2 large yellow (bell) peppers,
   quartered and seeded
 90ml/6 tbsp extra virgin olive oil
 2 sweet onions, thinly sliced
 1 garlic clove, thinly sliced
 5ml/1 tsp sugar
 4 tomatoes, peeled, seeded and
   roughly chopped
 2 bay leaves
 1 large fresh thyme sprig
 15ml/1 tbsp red verjuice or red wine

1 To make the peperonata, spread out the peppers on a board and brush the skin side with oil. Heat the remaining oil in a pan and add the onions and garlic. Fry over a medium-high heat for 6–8 minutes, or until lightly golden.

2 Prepare the barbecue. Heat a griddle on a grill rack over hot coals. Add the peppers, skin-side down. Lower the heat a little and grill them for 5 minutes until the skins are charred. Remove from the heat and put them under an upturned bowl. When cool enough to handle, rub off the skins and slice each piece into six or seven strips.

3 Add the pepper strips to the onion mixture, stir in the sugar and cook over a medium heat for about 2 minutes. Add the tomatoes and herbs and bring to the boil. Transfer the pan to the barbecue. Stir in the verjuice or wine, and simmer, uncovered, for about 30 minutes. Remove from the heat and cover to keep warm.

4 Meanwhile, soak eight wooden skewers with the bay leaf sprigs in a bowl of cold water for 30 minutes. Cut the fish into 12 large cubes and place in a bowl. Squeeze the juice from half a lime and half a lemon into a small bowl. Whisk in 45ml/3 tbsp of the oil. Cream the garlic and plenty of seasoning to a paste, add to the oil mixture and pour over the fish. Marinate for 30 minutes.

5 Cut the remaining lime and lemon halves into four wedges each. Using two skewers placed side by side instead of the usual one, thread alternately with three pieces of fish, one lime and one lemon wedge and two sprigs of bay leaves. Make three more brochettes in the same way.

6 Replace the griddle over a high heat and test that it is hot. Brush the brochettes with the remaining oil and grill for 3–4 minutes on each side, or until the fish is cooked through and nicely branded. Cover the kebabs and keep them warm for up to 5 minutes before serving with the peperonata in a little bowl on the side.

COOK'S TIPS
• The brochettes can also be cooked on an oiled grill rack over a medium to high heat. Cook for 8–10 minutes, turning the skewers several times, until the fish is cooked and the rind of the citrus fruits has begun to scorch.
• You may prefer to quickly re-heat the peperonata while keeping the kebabs warm.

Energy 426kcal/1777kJ; Protein 34g; Carbohydrate 22.2g, of which sugars 19.4g; Fat 22.6g, of which saturates 3.9g; Cholesterol 69mg; Calcium 53mg; Fibre 5.2g; Sodium 239mg.

GRIDDLED HALIBUT

ANY THICK WHITE FISH FILLETS CAN BE COOKED IN THIS VERSATILE DISH; TURBOT AND BRILL ARE ESPECIALLY DELICIOUS, BUT THE FLAVOURSOME SAUCE OF TOMATOES, CAPERS, ANCHOVIES AND HERBS ALSO GIVES HUMBLER FISH SUCH AS COD, HADDOCK OR HAKE A REAL LIFT.

SERVES FOUR

INGREDIENTS
- 2.5ml/½ tsp fennel seeds
- 2.5ml/½ tsp celery seeds
- 5ml/1 tsp mixed peppercorns
- 105ml/7 tbsp olive oil
- 5ml/1 tsp chopped fresh
  thyme leaves
- 5ml/1 tsp chopped fresh rosemary
  leaves
- 5ml/1 tsp chopped fresh oregano or
  marjoram leaves
- 675–800g/1½–1¾lb middle cut of
  halibut, about 3cm/1¼in thick, cut
  into 4 pieces
- coarse sea salt

For the sauce
- 105ml/7 tbsp extra virgin olive oil
- juice of 1 lemon
- 1 garlic clove, finely chopped
- 2 tomatoes, peeled, seeded
  and diced
- 5ml/1 tsp small capers
- 2 drained canned anchovy
  fillets, chopped
- 5ml/1 tsp chopped fresh chives
- 15ml/1 tbsp chopped fresh
  basil leaves
- 15ml/1 tbsp chopped fresh chervil

1 Prepare the barbecue. Heat a griddle on the grill rack over the hot coals. Mix the fennel and celery seeds with the peppercorns in a mortar. Crush with a pestle, and then stir in coarse sea salt to taste. Spoon the mixture into a shallow dish large enough to hold the fish in one layer and stir in the herbs and the olive oil.

2 Add the halibut pieces to the olive oil mixture, turning them to coat them thoroughly, then arrange them with the dark skin uppermost in the griddle. Cook for about 6–8 minutes, or until the fish is cooked all the way through and the skin has browned.

3 Combine all the sauce ingredients except the fresh herbs in a pan and heat gently on the grill rack until warm but not hot. Stir in the chives, basil and chervil.

4 Place the halibut on four warmed plates. Spoon the sauce around and over the fish and serve immediately.

Energy 363kcal/1513kJ; Protein 37.4g; Carbohydrate 1.9g, of which sugars 1.8g; Fat 22.9g, of which saturates 3.3g; Cholesterol 60mg; Calcium 82mg; Fibre 1.1g; Sodium 169mg.

SEA BASS WRAPPED IN VINE LEAVES

THIS DISH IS EFFORTLESS BUT MUST BE STARTED IN ADVANCE BECAUSE THE RICE NEEDS TO BE COLD BEFORE IT IS USED IN THE LITTLE PARCELS. ONCE THE FISH HAVE BEEN WRAPPED, ALL YOU HAVE TO DO IS KEEP THEM CHILLED, READY TO POP ON TO THE BARBECUE.

3 Season the sea bass fillets. Wash the vine leaves in water, then pat dry with kitchen paper. Lay each leaf in the centre of a double layer of foil. Top with a sea bass fillet. Divide the rice mixture among the fillets, spooning it towards one end. Fold the fillet over the rice, trickle over the remaining oil, lay the second vine leaf on top and bring the foil up around the fish and scrunch it together to seal. Chill the packages for up to 3 hours, or until needed.

4 Take the fish out of the refrigerator and prepare the barbecue. Position a lightly oiled grill rack over the hot coals. Place the parcels on the edge of the grill rack. Cook for 5 minutes over high heat, turning them around by 90 degrees halfway through. Open up the top of the foil a little and cook for 2 minutes more. Gently remove from the foil and transfer the vine parcels to individual plates and serve.

COOK'S TIP
For a quick salsa, chop half a seeded cucumber and half a pink onion. Place in a bowl and add 30ml/2 tbsp seasoned sushi vinegar and mix well. Add a little chilli to put a bit of a kick in it.

MAKES SIXTEEN

INGREDIENTS
90g/3½oz/½ cup Chinese black rice
400ml/14fl oz/1⅔ cups boiling water
45ml/3 tbsp extra virgin olive oil
1 small onion, chopped
1 fresh mild chilli, seeded and finely chopped
8 sea bass fillets, about 75g/3oz each, with skin
16 large fresh vine leaves
salt and ground black pepper

1 Place the Chinese black rice in a large pan. Add the measured boiling water and simmer for 15 minutes. Add a little salt to taste and simmer for a further 10 minutes, or until tender. Drain well and tip into a bowl.

2 Meanwhile, heat half the oil in a frying pan. Fry the onion gently for 5 minutes until softened but not browned. Add the chilli. Stir into the rice mixture and season with salt and pepper according to taste. Cool the rice completely and cover and chill until needed.

Energy 157kcal/656kJ; Protein 15.5g; Carbohydrate 9.9g, of which sugars 0.7g; Fat 6.1g, of which saturates 0.9g; Cholesterol 60mg; Calcium 105mg; Fibre 0.2g; Sodium 52mg.

SEA BASS WITH FENNEL

THE CLASSIC COMBINATION OF SEA BASS AND FENNEL WORKS PARTICULARLY WELL WHEN THE FISH IS COOKED OVER CHARCOAL. FENNEL TWIGS ARE TRADITIONALLY USED INSIDE THE FISH BUT THIS VERSION OF THE RECIPE USES FENNEL SEEDS, WHICH FLAVOUR THE FISH BEAUTIFULLY.

SERVES SIX

INGREDIENTS
   1 sea bass, about 1.3–1.6kg/
      3–3½lb, cleaned and scaled
   60ml/4 tbsp olive oil
   10ml/2 tsp fennel seeds
   2 large fennel bulbs
   60ml/4 tbsp Pernod
   salt and ground black pepper

1 Make four deep slashes in each side of the fish. Brush the fish with olive oil and season well with salt and freshly ground black pepper. Sprinkle the fennel seeds in the cavity and slashes of the fish.

2 Trim and slice the fennel bulbs thinly, reserving any leafy fronds to use as a garnish. Prepare the barbecue. Part the coals in the centre and position a drip tray. Position a lightly oiled grill rack over the hot coals. Put the fish inside a hinged wire grill or straight on to the grill rack over the drip tray. Cook over indirect medium heat using a cover, for 20 minutes, basting occasionally and turning once.

3 Meanwhile, brush the slices of fennel with olive oil and barbecue for about 8–10 minutes, turning the fennel occasionally, until tender. Remove the fish and fennel from the heat.

4 Scatter the fennel slices on a serving plate. Lay the fish on top and garnish with the reserved fennel fronds.

5 When ready for eating, heat the Pernod in a small pan on the side of the barbecue, light it and pour it, flaming, over the fish. Serve at once.

Energy 180kcal/750kJ; Protein 19.9g; Carbohydrate 1.2g, of which sugars 1.1g; Fat 8.1g, of which saturates 1.2g; Cholesterol 80mg; Calcium 146mg; Fibre 1.6g; Sodium 76mg.

SEARED TUNA WITH GINGER

THIS NORTH AFRICAN RECIPE IS UNBEATABLE FAST, NUTRITIOUS FARE FOR THE BARBECUE. TUNA STEAKS ARE RUBBED WITH HARISSA AND THEN GRIDDLED QUICKLY OVER HIGH HEAT AND SERVED WITH A DELICIOUS WARM SALAD SPICED WITH GINGER AND CHILLIES. NO MARINATING TIME IS NEEDED.

SERVES FOUR

INGREDIENTS

   30ml/2 tbsp olive oil
   5ml/1 tsp harissa
   5ml/1 tsp clear honey
   4 tuna steaks, about 200g/7oz each
   salt and ground black pepper
   lemon wedges, to serve
For the salad
   30ml/2 tbsp olive oil
   a little butter
   25g/1oz fresh root ginger, peeled and
     finely sliced
   2 garlic cloves, finely sliced
   2 green chillies, seeded and
     finely sliced
   6 spring onions (scallions), cut into
     bite size pieces
   2 large handfuls of watercress or
     rocket (arugula)
   juice of ½ lemon

1 Prepare the barbecue. While the coals are heating up, combine the olive oil, harissa, honey and salt in a bowl, and rub the mixture over the tuna steaks using your fingers.

2 Heat a griddle on the grill rack over hot coals. Sear the tuna steaks for about 2 minutes on each side. They should still be pink on the inside when pierced with a skewer.

3 Keep the tuna warm while you quickly prepare the salad: heat the olive oil and butter in a heavy pan on the side of the barbecue. Add the ginger, garlic, chillies and spring onions. Cook until the mixture begins to colour, then add the watercress or rocket. When it begins to wilt, toss in the lemon juice and season well.

4 Tip the warm salad on to a serving dish or individual plates. Slice the tuna steaks and arrange on top of the salad. Serve immediately with lemon wedges for squeezing over.

VARIATION
Prawns (shrimp) and scallops can be cooked in the same way. The shellfish will just need to be cooked briefly – too long and they will become rubbery.

Energy 176kcal/731kJ; Protein 12.3g; Carbohydrate 1.6g, of which sugars 1.6g; Fat 13.4g, of which saturates 2.2g; Cholesterol 14mg; Calcium 18mg; Fibre 0.4g; Sodium 25mg.

HAM-WRAPPED TROUT

SERRANO HAM IS USED TO STUFF AND WRAP TROUT FOR THIS UNUSUAL RECIPE FROM SPAIN, ENSURING A SUCCULENT FLAVOUR. ONE OF THE BEAUTIES OF THIS METHOD IS THAT THE SKINS COME OFF IN ONE PIECE, LEAVING THE SUCCULENT, MOIST FLESH TO BE EATEN WITH THE CRISPED, SALT HAM.

SERVES FOUR

INGREDIENTS
    4 brown or rainbow trout, about
        250g/9oz each, cleaned
    16 thin slices Serrano ham, about
        200g/7oz
    50g/2oz/¼ cup melted butter, plus
        extra for greasing
    salt and ground black pepper
    buttered potatoes, to
        serve (optional)

1 Extend the belly cavity of each trout, cutting up one side of the backbone. Slip a knife behind the rib bones to loosen them (sometimes just flexing the fish makes them pop up). Snip these off from both sides with scissors, and season the fish well inside.

2 Fold a piece of ham into each belly. Use smaller or broken bits of ham for this, and reserve the eight best slices.

COOK'S TIP
Serrano ham is a good choice for this recipe, as it is less fatty than prosciutto, which should help to avoid flare ups.

3 Prepare the barbecue. Position a lightly oiled grill rack over the hot coals. Brush each trout with a little butter, seasoning the outside lightly with salt and pepper. Wrap two ham slices round each one, crossways, tucking the ends into the belly.

4 Put the fish into oiled hinged wire fish baskets or directly on to the grill rack. The combined grilling time should be 4 minutes on each side, though it is wise to turn the fish every 2 minutes to ensure that the ham does not become charred.

5 Serve the trout hot, with the butter spooned over the top. Diners should open the trout on their plates, and eat them from the inside, pushing the flesh off the skin.

Energy 369kcal/1546kJ; Protein 48g; Carbohydrate 0.6g, of which sugars 0.6g; Fat 19.4g, of which saturates 8.8g; Cholesterol 216mg; Calcium 66mg; Fibre 0g; Sodium 821mg.

PAPRIKA-CRUSTED MONKFISH

SUCH A CHUNKY FISH AS MONKFISH IS JUST PERFECT FOR SKEWERING, AS IT IS NOT LIKELY TO
DISINTEGRATE BEFORE YOUR EYES AND FALL BETWEEN THE GRILL BARS AS YOU COOK. MONKFISH CAN
ALSO TAKE SOME STRONG FLAVOURS, SUCH AS THIS SMOKY PAPRIKA CRUST WITH CHORIZO.

SERVES FOUR

INGREDIENTS
1 monkfish tail, about 1kg/2¼lb,
  trimmed and filleted
10ml/2 tsp smoked red paprika
2 red (bell) peppers, halved
  and seeded
15ml/1 tbsp extra virgin olive oil
16 thin slices of chorizo
salt and ground black pepper
For the cucumber and mint sauce
150ml/¼ pint/⅔ cup Greek
  (US strained plain) yogurt
½ cucumber, halved lengthways
  and seeded
30ml/2 tbsp chopped fresh
  mint leaves

1 Place both monkfish fillets in a flat dish. Rub them all over with 5ml/1 tsp salt, then cover and leave in a cool place for 20 minutes. To make the sauce, pour the yogurt into a food processor. Cut the cucumber into it, season with a little salt and pulse to a pale green purée. Transfer to a serving bowl and stir in the mint.

2 Prepare the barbecue. Rinse the salt off the pieces of monkfish and lightly pat them dry with kitchen paper. Mix the smoked red paprika with a pinch of salt and gently rub the mixture evenly over the fish. Slice each pepper into 12 long strips and cut each monkfish fillet into ten equal pieces. Thread six pieces of pepper and five pieces of fish on to each of four long skewers and brush one side with a little extra virgin olive oil.

3 Position a lightly oiled grill rack over the hot coals. Grill the skewered food, oiled-side down over medium-high heat, for about 3½ minutes. Lightly brush the top side with oil, turn over and cook for 3–4 minutes more. Remove the skewers from the heat and keep warm.

4 Grill the chorizo slices for a second or two until just warm. Thread one piece of chorizo on to the end of each skewer and serve the rest alongside on individual plates. Serve with the prepared cucumber and mint sauce.

COOK'S TIP
If it is easier, fry the chorizo on a hot griddle set on the grill rack for 30 seconds on each side.

Energy 375kcal/1572kJ; Protein 51.7g; Carbohydrate 7.1g, of which sugars 6.8g; Fat 15.9g, of which saturates 5.6g; Cholesterol 57mg; Calcium 115mg; Fibre 2.1g; Sodium 445mg.

SWORDFISH WITH ROASTED TOMATOES

SUN-RIPENED TOMATOES ARE NATURALLY FULL OF FLAVOUR AND SWEETNESS, AND IN THIS MOROCCAN RECIPE THEY ARE ROASTED WITH SUGAR AND SPICES SO THAT THEY SIMPLY MELT IN THE MOUTH. AS AN ACCOMPANIMENT TO CHARGRILLED FISH OR POULTRY, THEY ARE SENSATIONAL.

SERVES FOUR

INGREDIENTS

1kg/2¼lb large vine or plum
  tomatoes, peeled, halved and seeded
5–10ml/1–2 tsp ground cinnamon
pinch of saffron threads
15ml/1 tbsp orange flower water
60ml/4 tbsp olive oil
45–60ml/3–4 tbsp sugar
4 swordfish steaks, about
  225g/8oz each
rind of ½ preserved lemon,
  finely chopped
small bunch of fresh coriander
  (cilantro), finely chopped
handful of blanched almonds
knob (pat) of butter
salt and ground black pepper

1 Preheat the oven to 110°C/225°F/ Gas ¼. Place the tomatoes on a baking sheet. Sprinkle with the cinnamon, saffron and orange flower water. Trickle half the oil over, being sure to moisten every tomato half, and sprinkle with sugar. Place the tray in the bottom of the oven and cook the tomatoes for about 3 hours, then turn the oven off and leave them to cool.

2 Prepare the barbecue. Heat a griddle on a grill rack over hot coals. Brush the remaining olive oil over the swordfish steaks and season with salt and pepper. Cook the steaks for 3–4 minutes on each side. Sprinkle the chopped preserved lemon rind and coriander over the steaks towards the end of the cooking time.

3 In a separate pan, fry the almonds in the butter until golden and sprinkle them over the tomatoes. Then serve the steaks immediately with the tomatoes.

VARIATIONS
If swordfish steaks are not available, tuna or shark steaks can be cooked in the same way with excellent results. Or, if you prefer, try the recipe with a lean sirloin or thinly cut fillet steak (beef tenderloin). The lemon and coriander flavours lift the meat beautifully.

Energy 463kcal/1941kJ; Protein 47.2g; Carbohydrate 19.9g, of which sugars 19.8g; Fat 22.2g, of which saturates 4.1g; Cholesterol 103mg; Calcium 59mg; Fibre 3.1g; Sodium 352mg.

MEAT AND POULTRY

It is surprising how many types and cuts of meat are
appropriate for successful barbecuing. Meat can be minced
and formed into koftas or burgers, or cut into chunks for
kebabs. As well as steaks, chops of all kinds are great
favourites for barbecuing, and are made even more
mouthwatering by the addition of fragrant marinades or a
herb butter. Chicken is also another popular barbecue meat,
and the reason is perhaps that it can be transformed in so
many ways by using different marinades or quick glazes.
Small portions are always popular because they cook quickly,
and the pages that follow contain examples of different
ways to prepare breast fillets, drumsticks, and achieve
exceptionally flavourful results. However, if you're planning
to feed a gathering of family and friends, and have a little
time to spare, you can also roast a whole chicken — even
without the aid of a rotisserie.

LAMB CUTLETS WITH LAVENDER

LAVENDER IS AN UNUSUAL FLAVOUR TO USE WITH MEAT, BUT ITS HEADY, SUMMERY SCENT WORKS WELL WITH BARBECUED LAMB. AS WELL AS ADDING LAVENDER TO THE MARINADE, YOU CAN SCATTER SPRIGS ON THE COALS OR GRILL RACK TO SMOKE. IF YOU PREFER, ROSEMARY CAN TAKE ITS PLACE.

SERVES FOUR

INGREDIENTS
4 racks of lamb, with 3–4
  cutlets each
1 shallot, finely chopped
45ml/3 tbsp chopped fresh lavender
15ml/1 tbsp balsamic vinegar
30ml/2 tbsp olive oil
15ml/1 tbsp lemon juice
salt and ground black pepper
handful of lavender sprigs

COOK'S TIP
You can ask your butcher to prepare
the cutlets for you.

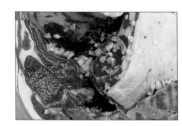

1 Prepare the barbecue. Position a lightly oiled grill rack over the hot coals. Place the racks of lamb in a wide dish and sprinkle over the chopped shallot so that each one is covered.

2 Sprinkle the chopped fresh lavender over the lamb racks.

3 Beat together the vinegar, olive oil and lemon juice, and pour them over the lamb. Season well with salt and pepper and then turn to coat evenly.

4 Scatter lavender sprigs over the grill rack or on the coals. Cook the lamb over medium-high heat for 15–20 minutes, turning once and basting with marinade, until golden brown on the outside and slightly pink in the centre.

Energy 565kcal/2333kJ; Protein 31.4g; Carbohydrate 1.2g, of which sugars 0.9g; Fat 48.3g, of which saturates 21.5g; Cholesterol 135mg; Calcium 26mg; Fibre 0.2g; Sodium 111mg.

LAMB KEBABS ᵂᴵᵀᴴ MINT CHUTNEY

THESE LITTLE ROUND LAMB KEBABS OWE THEIR EXOTIC FLAVOUR TO RAS EL HANOUT, A NORTH AFRICAN
SPICE WHOSE HEDONISTIC QUALITIES ARE ACHIEVED BY ADDING HIGHLY PERFUMED DRIED DAMASK
ROSE PETALS TO OVER TEN DIFFERENT SPICES. THE RESULT IS SUBLIME.

SERVES FOUR TO SIX

INGREDIENTS
30ml/2 tbsp extra virgin
  olive oil
1 onion, finely chopped
2 garlic cloves, crushed
35g/1¼oz/5 tbsp pine nuts
500g/1¼lb/2½ cups minced
  (ground) lamb
10ml/2 tsp ras el hanout spice mix
10ml/2 tsp dried pink rose petals
  (optional)
salt and ground black pepper
For the fresh mint chutney
40g/1½oz/1½ cups fresh
  mint leaves
10ml/2 tsp sugar
juice of 2 lemons
2 eating apples, peeled and
  finely grated
To serve (optional)
150ml/¼ pint/⅔ cup Greek
  (US strained plain) yogurt
7.5ml/1½ tsp rose harissa

1 If using wooden skewers, soak 18 in
cold water for 30 minutes. Heat the oil
in a frying pan on the stove. Add the
onion and garlic, and fry gently for
7 minutes. Stir in the pine nuts. Fry for
about 5 minutes more, or until the
mixture is slightly golden, then set aside
to cool.

2 Make the fresh mint chutney. Chop the
mint finely by hand or in a food processor,
then add the sugar, lemon juice and
grated apple. Stir or pulse to mix.

3 Prepare the barbecue. Place the
minced lamb in a large bowl and add
the ras el hanout and rose petals, if
using. Tip in the cooled onion mixture
and add salt and pepper. Using your
hands, mix well, then form into 18 balls.
Drain the skewers and mould a ball on
to each one. Once the flames have died
down, rake a few hot coals to one side.
Position a lightly oiled grill rack over the
hot coals.

4 Place the kebabs on the grill over the
part with the most coals to cook over
medium heat. If it is easier, cover the
barbecue with a lid or tented heavy-duty
foil so that the heat will circulate and
they will cook evenly all over. Otherwise,
you will need to stay with them, turning
them frequently for about 10 minutes.
This prevents the kebabs from forming
a hard crust before the meat is cooked
right through to the centre.

5 Serve with the yogurt, mixed with the
rose harissa, if you like. The kebabs can
also be wrapped in Middle Eastern flat
bread such as lavash with a green salad
and cucumber slices piled in with them.

COOK'S TIPS
• You can also cook these kebabs on a
hot griddle. They will take about
10 minutes. Sear on a high heat then
lower the heat and turn frequently.
• The dried pink rose petals can be
bought at Middle Eastern food stores.

Energy 257kcal/1070kJ; Protein 17.2g; Carbohydrate 5.1g, of which sugars 4.5g; Fat 18.8g, of which saturates 6g; Cholesterol 64mg; Calcium 33mg; Fibre 0.6g; Sodium 59mg.

GRILLED SKEWERED LAMB

IN GREECE, THIS SKEWERED LAMB DISH IS KNOWN AS SOUVLAKIA. TENDER LAMB IS MARINATED IN HERBS, OLIVE OIL AND LEMON JUICE AND THEN BARBECUED WITH SWEET PEPPERS AND RED ONIONS. THE SOUVLAKIA ARE AT THEIR BEST SERVED WITH TZATZIKI, A LARGE TOMATO SALAD AND BARBECUED BREAD.

SERVES FOUR

INGREDIENTS
  1 small shoulder of lamb, boned and
    with most of the fat removed
  2–3 onions, preferably red onions,
    quartered
  2 red or green (bell) peppers,
    quartered and seeded
  75ml/5 tbsp extra virgin olive oil
  juice of 1 lemon
  2 garlic cloves, crushed
  5ml/1 tsp dried oregano
  2.5ml/½ tsp dried thyme or some
    sprigs of fresh thyme, chopped
  salt and ground black pepper

1 Ask your butcher to trim the meat and cut it into 4cm/1½in cubes. (A little fat is desirable with souvlakia, because it keeps them moist and succulent during cooking.) Separate the onion quarters into pieces, each composed of two or three layers, and slice each pepper quarter in half widthways.

2 Put the oil, lemon juice, garlic and herbs in a large bowl. Season with salt and pepper, and whisk well to combine. Add the meat cubes, stirring to coat them in the mixture.

3 Cover the bowl tightly and leave to marinate for 4–8 hours in the refrigerator, stirring several times.

VARIATION
If you prefer, you can use 4–5 best end neck fillets instead of shoulder.

4 Lift out the meat cubes, reserving the marinade, and thread them on to long metal skewers, alternating each piece of meat with a piece of pepper and a piece of onion. Lay them across a grill pan or baking tray and brush them with the reserved marinade.

5 Prepare the barbecue. Position a lightly oiled grill rack over the hot coals. Cook the souvlakia over medium-high heat for 10 minutes, or until they start to get scorched. Turn the skewers over, brush them again with the marinade (or a little olive oil) and cook them for 10–15 minutes more. Serve the souvlakia immediately.

COOK'S TIP
Although these souvlakia cook best with a little fat left on the meat, always be sure to trim excess fat from meats that are to be barbecued, as the fat will drip on to the coals and can cause flare-ups.

Energy 419kcal/1743kJ; Protein 32.3g; Carbohydrate 16.3g, of which sugars 13.1g; Fat 25.4g, of which saturates 8.4g; Cholesterol 138mg; Calcium 51mg; Fibre 3.4g; Sodium 89mg.

MOROCCAN SPICED LAMB

THIS MOROCCAN SPECIALITY OFTEN CONSISTS OF A WHOLE LAMB GRILLED SLOWLY OVER A CHARCOAL FIRE FOR MANY HOURS. THIS VERSION IS FOR A LARGE SHOULDER, RUBBED WITH SPICES AND CHARGRILLED. WHEN COOKED, THE MEAT IS HACKED OFF AND DIPPED IN ROASTED SALT AND CUMIN.

SERVES FOUR TO SIX

INGREDIENTS
    1 shoulder of lamb, about 1.8kg/4lb
    4 garlic cloves, crushed
    15ml/1 tbsp paprika
    15ml/1 tbsp freshly ground
      cumin seeds
    105ml/7 tbsp extra virgin olive oil
    45–60ml/3–4 tbsp finely chopped
      mint leaves
    a few sturdy thyme sprigs,
      for basting
    salt and ground black pepper
To serve
    45ml/3 tbsp cumin seeds
    25ml/1½ tbsp coarse sea salt

1 Open up the natural pockets in the lamb, and stuff with the garlic. Mix the paprika, ground cumin and seasoning, and rub all over the shoulder. Cover and leave the lamb for about 1 hour. Mix the oil and mint in a bowl for basting the meat during roasting.

2 Prepare a barbecue. Once the flames have died down, rake the hot coals to one side and insert a drip tray flat beside them. Position a lightly oiled grill rack over the hot coals.

3 Place the lamb shoulder on the grill rack over medium-high heat and directly over the drip tray. Cover with a lid or tented heavy-duty foil. For the initial 30 minutes turn the meat frequently, basting using the thyme branches and mint oil. Then roast the joint for a further 2 hours, turning and basting every 15 minutes so that it remains moist.

4 If you need to replenish the coals, do so before the heat is too low. It will take about 10 minutes to heat sufficiently to continue the cooking.

5 Dry-roast the cumin seeds and coarse salt for 2 minutes in a heavy frying pan. Do not let them burn. Tip them into a mortar and pound with the pestle until roughly ground.

6 When the meat is cooked, remove from the barbecue, wrap in double foil and rest it for 15 minutes. Serve sliced with the roasted cumin seeds and salt for dipping.

Energy 618kcal/2564kJ; Protein 42.7g; Carbohydrate 0.8g, of which sugars 0.1g; Fat 49.3g, of which saturates 21.2g; Cholesterol 183mg; Calcium 16mg; Fibre 0.2g; Sodium 150mg.

BASIL AND PECORINO STUFFED PORK

THIS IS A VERY EASY DISH TO MAKE AND LOOKS EXTREMELY IMPRESSIVE. IT IS GOOD FOR A BULK COOKOUT, BECAUSE YOU CAN GET SEVERAL FILLETS ON A BARBECUE GRILL, AND EACH ONE YIELDS ABOUT EIGHT CHUNKY SLICES. SERVE WITH A CHICKPEA AND ONION SALAD.

SERVES SIX TO EIGHT

INGREDIENTS
2 pork fillets (tenderloins), each
  about 350g/12oz
45ml/3 tbsp olive oil
40g/1½oz/1½ cups fresh basil
  leaves, chopped
50g/2oz Pecorino cheese, grated
2.5ml/½ tsp chilli flakes
salt and ground black pepper

COOK'S TIP
• If you don't use a lid and drip tray, move the coals so there are less on one side than the other. Move the pork during cooking to prevent burning.
• Pork fillets are incredibly versatile and perfect for the barbecue. Not only can they be exquisitely stuffed, but the large suface area, and the fact that they are cooked on all sides, makes for exceptionally flavourful meat dishes.

1 Make a 1cm/½in slit down the length of one of the fillets. Continue to slice, cutting along the fold of the meat, until you can open it out flat. Lay between two sheets of baking parchment and pound with a rolling pin to an even thickness of about 1cm/½in. Lift off the top sheet of parchment and brush the meat with a little oil. Press half the basil leaves on to the surface, then scatter over half the Pecorino cheese and chilli flakes. Add a little black pepper.

2 Roll up lengthways to form a sausage and tie with kitchen string (twine). Repeat with the second fillet. Put them in a shallow bowl with the remaining oil, cover and put in a cool place until ready to cook.

3 Prepare the barbecue. Twenty minutes before you are ready to cook, season the meat with salt. Wipe any excess oil off the meat. Once the flames have died down, rake the hot coals to one side and insert a drip tray beside them. Position a lightly oiled grill rack over the hot coals.

4 Put the tenderloins on to the grill rack over high heat, directly over the coals. Grill for 5 minutes over the coals, turning to sear on all sides, then move them over the drip tray and grill for 15 minutes more. Cover with a lid or tented heavy-duty foil, and turn them over from time to time. When done, remove and wrap in foil. Leave to rest for 10 minutes before slicing into rounds and serving.

Energy 174kcal/725kJ; Protein 21.3g; Carbohydrate 0.1g, of which sugars 0.1g; Fat 9.7g, of which saturates 3.1g; Cholesterol 61mg; Calcium 91mg; Fibre 0.3g; Sodium 131mg.

PORK CHOPS <u>WITH</u> FIELD MUSHROOMS

LEMON GRASS AND TYPICAL AROMATIC THAI FLAVOURINGS MAKE A SUPERB MARINADE FOR PORK CHOPS,
WHICH ARE ACCOMPANIED BY A FIERY SAUCE THAT IS SIMPLY PUT TOGETHER IN A PAN ON THE BARBECUE
GRILL RACK. SERVE WITH THE BARBECUED MUSHROOMS, A SALAD AND CRUSTY BREAD.

<u>SERVES FOUR</u>

INGREDIENTS
 4 pork chops
 4 large field (portobello) mushrooms
 45ml/3 tbsp vegetable oil
 4 fresh red chillies, seeded and
  thinly sliced
 45ml/3 tbsp Thai fish sauce
 90ml/6 tbsp fresh lime juice
 4 shallots, chopped
 5ml/1 tsp roasted ground rice
 30ml/2 tbsp spring onions
  (scallions), chopped, plus shredded
  spring onions to garnish
 coriander (cilantro) leaves, to garnish
For the marinade
 2 garlic cloves, chopped
 15ml/1 tbsp sugar
 15ml/1 tbsp Thai fish sauce
 30ml/2 tbsp soy sauce
 15ml/1 tbsp sesame oil
 15ml/1 tbsp whisky or dry sherry
 2 lemon grass stalks, finely chopped
 2 spring onions (scallions), chopped

1 To make the marinade, combine the garlic, sugar, sauces, oil and whisky or sherry in a large, shallow dish. Stir in the lemon grass and spring onions.

2 Add the pork chops, turning to coat them in the marinade. Cover and leave to marinate for 1–2 hours. Prepare the barbecue. Position a lightly oiled grill rack over the hot coals.

3 Lift the chops out of the marinade and place them on the grill rack. Cook over high heat for 5–7 minutes on each side. Brush with the marinade during cooking up until the final 5 minutes of cooking. Meanwhile, brush both sides of the mushrooms with 15ml/1 tbsp of the oil and cook them for about 2 minutes without turning.

4 Heat the remaining oil in a wok or small frying pan on the grill rack, then remove the pan from the heat and stir in the chillies, fish sauce, lime juice, shallots, ground rice and chopped spring onions. Put the pork chops and mushrooms on a large serving plate and spoon over the sauce. Garnish with the coriander leaves and shredded spring onion.

Energy 408kcal/1705kJ; Protein 49.7g; Carbohydrate 9.8g, of which sugars 8.3g; Fat 19.1g, of which saturates 4.9g; Cholesterol 123mg; Calcium 62mg; Fibre 2g; Sodium 1176mg.

PORK SCHNITZEL

THIN PORK ESCALOPES ARE IDEAL FOR ROLLING AROUND A RICHLY FLAVOURED STUFFING AND THEN BARBECUED IN THIS VARIATION OF A CROATIAN RECIPE. SERVE THEM WITH A CREAMY SAUCE FLAVOURED WITH MUSHROOMS AND BACON, AND SOME COUNTRY-STYLE CRUSTY BREAD FOR MOPPING UP JUICES.

3 Divide the livers evenly between the four prepared pork steaks and roll up into neat parcels. Secure with cocktail sticks or string.

4 To make the sauce, fry the onion, bacon and mushrooms in the oil for 2–3 minutes, then add the mustard, white wine and sour cream. Stir to simmering point, then add the double cream and season.

SERVES FOUR

INGREDIENTS
    4 pork leg steaks or escalopes (US
      pork scallop), about 200g/7oz each
    60ml/4 tbsp olive oil
    115g/4oz chicken livers, chopped
    1 garlic clove, crushed
    salt and ground black pepper
    15ml/1 tbsp chopped fresh parsley,
      to garnish
For the sauce
    1 onion, thinly sliced
    115g/4oz streaky (fatty) bacon,
      thinly sliced
    175g/6oz/2 cups sliced mixed
      wild mushrooms
    120ml/4fl oz/½ cup olive oil
    5ml/1 tsp ready-made mustard
    150ml/¼ pint/⅔ cup white wine
    120ml/4fl oz/½ cup sour cream
    250ml/8fl oz/1 cup double
      (heavy) cream

1 Soak 8 cocktail sticks (toothpicks) in water for 30 minutes. Place each pork steak between 2 sheets of dampened clear film (plastic wrap) or baking parchment and flatten with a meat mallet or rolling pin until about 15 x 10cm/6 x 4in. Season well.

2 Heat half the oil in a frying pan and cook the chicken livers and garlic for 1–2 minutes. Remove, drain on kitchen paper and leave to cool.

5 Prepare the barbecue. Position a lightly oiled grill rack over the hot coals. Brush the pork rolls with oil and cook over medium heat for 8–10 minutes on each side, brushing with oil as necessary, until golden brown.

6 Reheat the sauce over the barbecue. Remove the cocktail sticks or string from the rolls. Serve the schnitzels with the sauce and garnish with a little parsley.

COOK'S TIP
Veal or chicken breast fillet would also work well with this recipe.

Energy 969kcal/4009kJ; Protein 50.2g; Carbohydrate 3.8g, of which sugars 3.3g; Fat 81.6g, of which saturates 33.7g; Cholesterol 248mg; Calcium 83mg; Fibre 0.7g; Sodium 532mg.

STILTON BURGERS

A VARIATION ON THE TRADITIONAL BURGER, THIS TASTY RECIPE CONTAINS A DELICIOUS SURPRISE: A CREAMY FILLING OF LIGHTLY MELTED STILTON CHEESE. HOME-MADE BURGERS ARE QUITE QUICK TO MAKE AND TASTE SUPERIOR TO BOUGHT ONES. CHOOSE GOOD QUALITY BEEF FOR THE BEST FLAVOUR.

SERVES FOUR

INGREDIENTS
    450g/1lb/2 cups minced
      (ground) beef
    1 onion, chopped
    1 celery stick, chopped
    5ml/1 tsp dried mixed herbs
    5ml/1 tsp prepared mustard
    50g/2oz/½ cup crumbled
      Stilton cheese
    4 burger buns
    salt and ground black pepper

3 Shape and flatten the remaining four portions and place on top. Use your hands to mould the rounds together, encasing the crumbled cheese, and shaping them into four burgers.

4 Cook over medium-high heat for about 5 minutes on each side. Split the burger buns and place a burger inside each. Serve with salad and mustard pickle, if you like.

1 Prepare the barbecue. Position a lightly oiled grill rack over the hot coals. Mix the minced beef with the onion, celery, mixed herbs and mustard. Season well with salt and pepper, and bring together with your hands to form a firm mixture.

2 Divide the mixture into eight equal portions. Shape four portions into rounds and flatten each one slightly. Place a little of the crumbled cheese in the centre of each round.

Energy 428kcal/1789kJ; Protein 29.6g; Carbohydrate 25.9g, of which sugars 2.2g; Fat 23.5g, of which saturates 10.7g; Cholesterol 79mg; Calcium 113mg; Fibre 1.1g; Sodium 454mg.

STEAK CIABATTA

THIS ALL-TIME FAVOURITE TASTES ALL THE BETTER WHEN ENJOYED ON A BEACH AFTER AN AFTERNOON SPENT BATTLING THE SURF.

SERVES FOUR

INGREDIENTS
  2 romaine or cos lettuces
  3 garlic cloves, crushed to a paste
    with enough salt to season
    the steaks
  30ml/2 tbsp extra virgin olive oil
  4 sirloin steaks, 2.5cm/1in thick,
    total weight about 900g/2lb
  4 small ciabatta rolls
  salt and ground black pepper
For the dressing
  10ml/2 tsp Dijon mustard
  5ml/1 tsp cider or white wine vinegar
  15ml/1 tbsp olive oil

2 Mix the garlic and oil together in a shallow dish. Add the steaks and rub the mixture into both surfaces. Cover and leave in a cool place until ready to cook.

1 Separate the lettuce leaves and clean them. Put into an airtight container until ready to use. Make a dressing for the salad by mixing the mustard and vinegar in a small jar. Gradually whisk in the oil, then season to taste.

3 Prepare the barbecue. Position a lightly oiled grill rack over the hot coals. Transfer the steaks to the grill rack. For rare meat, cook the steaks for 2 minutes on one side, without moving, then turn over and grill the other side for 3 minutes. For medium steaks, cook for 4 minutes on each side. Transfer to a plate, cover loosely and leave to rest for 2 minutes.

4 Dress the lettuce leaves. Split each ciabatta. Place the ciabatta cut-side down on the grill rack for a minute to heat. Slice the steaks and arrange on top of the ciabatta, with some of the leaves. Replace the lids and cut each filled ciabatta in half to serve.

COOK'S TIP
A steak sandwich is also delicious spread with hummus. Follow the classic hummus recipe given in the Side Dishes and Accompaniments chapter.

Energy 665kcal/2796kJ; Protein 64g; Carbohydrate 53.5g, of which sugars 4.4g; Fat 23.2g, of which saturates 6.4g; Cholesterol 115mg; Calcium 158mg; Fibre 3g; Sodium 698mg

INDONESIAN BEEF BURGERS

THIS UNUSUAL INDONESIAN RECIPE CONTAINS COCONUT, WHICH GIVES THE BURGERS A RICH AND SUCCULENT FLAVOUR. THEY TASTE GREAT WITH A SHARP YET SWEET MANGO CHUTNEY AND CAN BE EATEN IN MINI NAAN OR PITTA BREADS.

MAKES EIGHT

INGREDIENTS
    500g/1¼lb/2½ cups minced
      (ground) beef
    5ml/1 tsp anchovy paste
    10ml/2 tsp tomato purée (paste)
    10ml/2 tsp ground coriander
    5ml/1 tsp ground cumin
    7.5ml/1½ tsp finely grated fresh
      root ginger
    2 garlic cloves, crushed
    1 egg white
    75g/3oz solid creamed coconut,
      grated or 40g/1½oz desiccated (dry
      unsweetened shredded) coconut
    45ml/3 tbsp chopped fresh
      coriander (cilantro)
    salt and ground black pepper
    8 fresh vine leaves (optional),
      to serve

1 Mix the minced beef, anchovy paste, tomato purée, coriander, cumin, ginger and garlic in a bowl. Add the egg white, with salt and pepper to taste. Mix well using your hands. Add the grated coconut and work it gently into the meat mixture so that it doesn't melt, or stir in the desiccated coconut. Add the fresh coriander.

2 Divide into eight pieces and form chunky burgers, about 7.5cm/3in in diameter. Chill for 30 minutes.

3 Prepare the barbecue. Once the flames have died down, rake the hot coals to one side and insert a drip tray beside them. Position a lightly oiled grill rack over the hot coals. Cook the chilled burgers over medium-high heat directly over the drip tray for 10–15 minutes, turning them over once or twice. Check they are cooked by breaking off a piece of one of the burgers.

4 If you are using the vine leaves, wash them and pat dry with kitchen paper. Wrap one around each burger. Serve with mango chutney and mini naan or pitta breads.

Energy 177kcal/734kJ; Protein 13.4g; Carbohydrate 0.8g, of which sugars 0.7g; Fat 13.4g, of which saturates 7g; Cholesterol 38mg; Calcium 22mg; Fibre 1.1g; Sodium 90mg.

SPICY BEEF KOFTAS WITH CHICKPEA PURÉE

*WHEREVER YOU GO IN THE MIDDLE EAST YOU WILL ENCOUNTER THESE TASTY KEBABS, AS STREET
FOOD, ON BARBECUES, AT BEACH BARS AND AT FAMILY MEALS. CHICKPEA PURÉE IS THE TRADITIONAL
ACCOMPANIMENT, AND A MIXED SALAD WILL ALSO GO WELL WITH THE RICH FLAVOURS.*

SERVES SIX

INGREDIENTS

500g/1¼lb/2½ cups finely minced
   (ground) beef
1 onion, grated
10ml/2 tsp ground cumin
10ml/2 tsp ground coriander
10ml/2 tsp paprika
4ml/¾ tsp cayenne pepper
5ml/1 tsp salt
small bunch of fresh flat leaf parsley,
   finely chopped
small bunch of fresh coriander
   (cilantro), finely chopped
For the chickpea purée
225g/8oz/1¼ cups dried chickpeas,
   soaked overnight, drained and
   cooked until soft
50ml/2fl oz/¼ cup olive oil
juice of 1 lemon
2 garlic cloves, crushed
5ml/1 tsp cumin seeds
30ml/2 tbsp light tahini paste
60ml/4 tbsp thick Greek (US strained
   plain) yogurt
40g/1½oz/3 tbsp butter, melted
salt and ground black pepper
salad and bread, to serve

1 Mix the minced beef with the onion,
cumin, ground coriander, paprika,
cayenne, salt, parsley and fresh
coriander. Knead the mixture well, then
pound it until smooth in a mortar with a
pestle or in a blender or food processor.
Place the minced beef mixture in a dish
then cover and leave to stand in a cool
place for 1 hour.

2 Meanwhile, make the chickpea purée.
Preheat the oven to 200°C/400°F/Gas 6.
In a blender or food processor, process
the chickpeas with the olive oil, lemon
juice, garlic, cumin seeds, tahini and
yogurt until well mixed. Season with salt
and pepper, tip the purée into an
ovenproof dish, cover with foil and heat
through in the oven for 20 minutes.
Prepare the barbecue. Position a lightly
oiled grill rack over the hot coals.

3 Divide the meat mixture into six
portions. Gently squeeze and pat the
meat mixture into shape along each of
six skewers so that it is quite thick and
resembles a fat sausage. Cook the
koftas over high heat for 4–5 minutes
on each side.

4 Melt the butter in a small pan on the
barbecue and pour it over the hot
chickpea purée. Serve the koftas with
the hot chickpea purée, a mixed salad
and bread.

Energy 449kcal/1870kJ; Protein 26.3g; Carbohydrate 20.5g, of which sugars 2.5g; Fat 29.7g, of which saturates 10.7g; Cholesterol 64mg; Calcium 141mg; Fibre 5g; Sodium 134mg.

VEAL CHOPS WITH BASIL BUTTER

SUCCULENT VEAL CHOPS FROM THE LOIN ARE AN EXPENSIVE CUT AND ARE BEST COOKED QUICKLY AND SIMPLY. THE FLAVOUR OF BASIL GOES PARTICULARLY WELL WITH VEAL, BUT OTHER HERBS CAN BE USED INSTEAD IF YOU PREFER. SERVE WITH BARBECUED VEGETABLES OR A SALAD.

SERVES TWO

INGREDIENTS

25g/1oz/2 tbsp butter, softened
15ml/1 tbsp Dijon mustard
15ml/1 tbsp chopped fresh basil
olive oil, for brushing
2 veal loin chops, 2.5cm/1in thick,
   about 225g/8oz each
salt and ground black pepper
fresh basil sprigs, to garnish

COOK'S TIP

Chilled herb butters make perfect impromptu sauces for cooked meats and fish. Basil butter is a firm favourite, but other fresh herbs such as chives, tarragon and parsley also work well.

1 To make the basil butter, cream the softened butter with the Dijon mustard and chopped fresh basil in a large mixing bowl, then season with plenty of freshly ground black pepper.

2 Prepare the barbecue. Position a lightly oiled grill rack over the hot coals.

3 Brush both sides of each chop with olive oil and season with a little salt. Cook the chops over high heat for 7–10 minutes, basting with oil and turning once, until done to your liking.

4 Top each chop with basil butter and serve at once, garnished with basil.

Energy 718kcal/3017kJ; Protein 113.8g; Carbohydrate 0.3g, of which sugars 0.0g; Fat 29.13g, of which saturates 16.0g; Cholesterol 3135mg; Calcium 35mg; Fibre 0.3g; Sodium 448mg.

VENISON CHOPS WITH ROMESCO SAUCE

ROMESCO IS THE CATALAN WORD FOR THE ÑORA CHILLI. IT LENDS A SPICY ROUNDNESS TO ONE OF SPAIN'S GREATEST SAUCES, FROM TARRAGONA. THE SAUCE ALSO CONTAINS GROUND TOASTED NUTS AND OFTEN ANOTHER FIERCER CHILLI. IT CAN BE SERVED HOT, AS HERE, OR COLD AS A DIP FOR VEGETABLES.

SERVES FOUR

INGREDIENTS

    4 venison chops, cut 2cm/¾in thick
       and about 175–200g/6–7oz each
    30ml/2 tbsp olive oil
    50g/2oz/¼ cup butter
For the *romesco* sauce
    3 *ñora* chillies
    1 hot dried chilli
    25g/1oz/¼ cup almonds
    150ml/¼ pint/⅔ cup olive oil
    1 slice stale bread, crusts removed
    3 garlic cloves, chopped
    3 tomatoes, peeled, seeded and
       roughly chopped
    60ml/4 tbsp sherry vinegar
    60ml/4 tbsp red wine vinegar
    salt and ground black pepper

1 To make the *romesco* sauce, slit both types of chilli and remove the seeds, then leave the chillies to soak in warm water for about 30 minutes until soft. Drain the chillies, dry them on kitchen paper and chop finely.

2 Dry-fry the almonds in a frying pan over a medium heat, shaking the pan occasionally, until the nuts are toasted evenly. Transfer the nuts to a food processor or blender.

3 Add 45ml/3 tbsp of the oil to the frying pan and fry the bread slice until golden on both sides. Lift it out with a slotted spoon and drain on kitchen paper. Tear the bread and add to the food processor or blender. Fry the chopped garlic in the oil remaining in the pan.

COOK'S TIP
Always be careful when preparing chillies, as the juice can irritate cuts or the eyes if it touches them. Wear rubber gloves during preparation or rub olive oil over the fingers before preparation and then scrub hands thoroughly afterwards.

4 Add the soaked chillies and tomatoes to the processor or blender. Tip in the garlic, with the oil from the pan, and blend the mixture to form a smooth paste.

5 With the motor running, gradually add the remaining olive oil and then the vinegars. When the sauce is smooth and well blended, scrape it into a bowl and season with salt and ground black pepper to taste. Cover with clear film (plastic wrap) and chill for 2 hours. Transfer to a small pan.

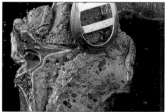

6 Prepare the barbecue. Position a lightly oiled grill rack over the hot coals. Melt the butter with the oil in a small pan on the grill rack and use to brush over the chops. Cook the chops for 5–6 minutes on each side until golden brown and cooked through.

7 Meanwhile, heat the *romesco* sauce gently. If it is too thick, stir in a little boiling water. Serve the sauce with the chops, accompanied by vegetables or salad.

Energy 531kcal/2206kJ; Protein 30.3g; Carbohydrate 6g, of which sugars 2.9g; Fat 43.9g, of which saturates 11.8g; Cholesterol 89mg; Calcium 43mg; Fibre 1.5g; Sodium 185mg.

BARBECUED CHICKEN SALAD

THIS DISH IS REMARKABLY SIMPLE BUT TASTES ABSOLUTELY WONDERFUL. SIMPLY BARBECUED CHICKEN IS TOSSED IN A CRISP SALAD OF BABY SPINACH AND CHERRY TOMATOES WITH A HERBY AND NUTTY DRESSING. THIS WOULD MAKE A SUPER FILLING TO POP INTO WARMED AND SPLIT PITTA BREADS.

SERVES FOUR

INGREDIENTS

30ml/2 tbsp olive oil, plus extra
    for brushing
30ml/2 tbsp hazelnut oil
15ml/1 tbsp white wine vinegar
1 garlic clove, crushed
15ml/1 tbsp chopped fresh
    mixed herbs
225g/8oz baby spinach leaves
250g/9oz cherry tomatoes, halved
1 bunch spring onions
    (scallions), chopped
2 skinless chicken breast fillets
salt and ground black pepper

COOK'S TIP
Remember to cut up your cooked chicken on a different plate to that which held the raw chicken, as it is essential to avoid cross-contamination when cooking meat or poultry.

1 First make the dressing. Place 30ml/ 2 tbsp of the olive oil, the hazelnut oil, vinegar, garlic and herbs in a small bowl or jug (pitcher) and whisk together until thoroughly mixed. Set the dressing aside.

2 Trim any long stalks from the spinach leaves and discard, then place the leaves in a large serving bowl with the tomatoes and spring onions, and toss together to mix.

3 Prepare the barbecue. Position a lightly oiled grill rack over the hot coals. Brush the chicken breasts all over with oil and then grill them over medium heat for 15–20 minutes, turning regularly, until cooked through and golden brown. Brush them with oil if necessary during cooking to keep them moist. Cut the chicken into thin slices.

4 Scatter the chicken pieces over the salad, give the dressing a quick whisk to blend, then drizzle it over the salad and gently toss all the ingredients together to mix. Season to taste and serve immediately.

VARIATION
You can try out different dressings for this salad. For example, try a piquant combination of 20ml/4 tsp olive oil, 15ml/1 tbsp balsamic vinegar, 10ml/ 2 tsp honey and 30ml/2 tbsp mustard.

Energy 436kcal/1830kJ; Protein 37.3g; Carbohydrate 34.6g, of which sugars 12.8g; Fat 17.5g, of which saturates 4.6g; Cholesterol 105mg; Calcium 96mg; Fibre 3.9g; Sodium 194mg.

STUFFED CORN-FED CHICKEN

THIS IS ONE OF THOSE DISHES THAT IS IDEAL TO COOK FOR FRIENDS. IT DOES NOT REQUIRE ANY EFFORT BUT LOOKS AND TASTES AS IF YOU HAVE GONE TO HUGE AMOUNTS OF TROUBLE. SERVE GRILLED MEDITERRANEAN VEGETABLES, OR USE SIMPLY DRESSED SALAD LEAVES WITH THE CHICKEN.

SERVES FOUR TO SIX

INGREDIENTS

  4–6 chicken breast fillets, preferably
    from a corn-fed bird
  115g/4oz firm goat's cheese
  60ml/4 tbsp chopped fresh oregano
  20ml/4 tsp maple syrup
  juice of 1 lemon
  oil, for brushing
  salt and ground black pepper

1 Slash a pocket horizontally in each chicken fillet. Mix the goat's cheese, chopped oregano and 10ml/2 tsp of the maple syrup in a small bowl. Stuff the pockets in the chicken with the mixture. Don't overfill.

2 Put the remaining maple syrup into a shallow dish large enough to hold the chicken fillets in a single layer. Stir in the lemon juice and add the chicken fillets. Rub them all over with the maple syrup mixture, then cover and leave in a cool place for 20 minutes, turning them occasionally. Season with salt and pepper and marinate for 10 minutes more.

3 Prepare the barbecue. Once the flames have died down, rake the hot coals to one side and insert a drip tray flat beside them. Position a lightly oiled grill rack over the hot coals. Lay the chicken breast portions, skin-side up, on the grill rack over the drip tray. Cover with a lid or tented heavy-duty foil.

4 Grill the chicken over high heat for about 15 minutes in total, turning and moving the pieces around the grill rack so that they cook evenly without getting too charred. Baste with any remaining marinade 5 minutes before the end of cooking.

5 Transfer the chicken to a dish to rest and keep warm for about 5 minutes before serving.

COOK'S TIP
You can cook these successfully on a hot griddle. They will take about 20 minutes. Sear on a high heat then lower the heat. Turn frequently.

Energy 180kcal/756kJ; Protein 28.3g; Carbohydrate 3g, of which sugars 3g; Fat 6.1g, of which saturates 3.7g; Cholesterol 88mg; Calcium 44mg; Fibre 0.3g; Sodium 186mg.

CHARGRILLED CHICKEN WITH PEPPERS

CHICKEN REALLY LENDS ITSELF TO IMAGINATIVE MARINADES USING ALL KINDS OF AROMATIC INGREDIENTS. HERE FRENCH MUSTARD, GARLIC AND CHILLIES MAKE A PIQUANT COMBINATION THAT TASTES REALLY GREAT ON THE CHICKEN AS WELL AS THE ACCOMPANYING PEPPERS AND TOMATOES.

2 Beat together all the marinade ingredients in a large bowl. Add the chicken pieces and turn them over to coat them thoroughly in the marinade. Cover the bowl with clear film (plastic wrap) and place in the refrigerator for 4–8 hours, turning the chicken pieces over in the marinade a couple of times.

3 Prepare the barbecue. Position a lightly oiled grill rack over the hot coals. Transfer the chicken pieces to the grill. Add the pepper pieces and the tomatoes to the marinade and set it aside for 15 minutes. Grill the chicken pieces for 20–25 minutes over medium heat. Watch them closely and move them away from the area where the heat is most fierce if they start to burn.

SERVES FOUR TO SIX

INGREDIENTS
1½ chickens, total weight about
  2.25kg/5lb, jointed, or
  12 chicken pieces
2–3 red or green (bell) peppers,
  quartered and seeded
4–5 tomatoes, halved horizontally
lemon wedges, to serve
For the marinade
  90ml/6 tbsp extra virgin olive oil
  juice of 1 large lemon
  5ml/1 tsp French mustard
  4 garlic cloves, crushed
  2 fresh red or green chillies, seeded
  and chopped
  5ml/1 tsp dried oregano
  salt and ground black pepper

1 If you are jointing the chicken yourself, divide the legs into two. Make a couple of slits in the deepest part of the flesh of each piece of chicken, using a small sharp knife. This will help the marinade to be absorbed more efficiently and allow the chicken to cook thoroughly.

COOK'S TIP
You can, of course, cook these chicken pieces indoors under the grill (broiler). Have the heat fairly high, but don't place the chicken too close to the source. They will probably need less time than when cooked over the coals – allow about 15 minutes each side.

4 Turn the chicken pieces over and cook them for 20–25 minutes more. Meanwhile, thread the peppers on two long metal skewers. Add them to the barbecue grill, with the tomatoes, for the last 15 minutes of cooking. Remember to keep an eye on them and turn them over at least once. Serve with the lemon wedges.

Energy 337kcal/1419kJ; Protein 57.6g; Carbohydrate 7.2g, of which sugars 6.9g; Fat 8.7g, of which saturates 1.6g; Cholesterol 163mg; Calcium 48mg; Fibre 2.5g; Sodium 154mg.

SMOKED CHICKEN WITH BUTTERNUT PESTO

WHOLE CHICKEN SMOKED OVER HICKORY WOOD CHIPS ACQUIRES A PERFECTLY TANNED SKIN AND SUCCULENT PINKISH FLESH. THE BUTTERNUT SQUASH ROASTS ALONGSIDE IT, WRAPPED IN FOIL, AND IS LATER TRANSFORMED INTO A DELICIOUS PESTO. THE CHICKEN ALSO TASTES GREAT COLD.

SERVES FOUR TO SIX

INGREDIENTS

1.3kg/3lb roasting chicken
1 lemon, quartered
8–10 fresh bay leaves
3 branches fresh rosemary
15ml/1 tbsp olive oil
salt and ground black pepper
4 handfuls hickory wood chips
   soaked in cold water for at least
   30 minutes
For the pesto
1 butternut squash, about
   675g/1½lb, halved and seeded
2 garlic cloves, sliced
2 fresh thyme sprigs
45ml/3 tbsp olive oil
25g/1oz/⅓ cup freshly grated
   Parmesan cheese

1 Prepare the barbecue. Cut away any excess fat from the opening to the chicken cavity, season the inside and stuff with lemon quarters, bay leaves and sprigs from one rosemary branch. Tie the legs together with kitchen string (twine) and rub the bird all over with the oil. Season the skin lightly.

2 Prepare the butternut squash for the pesto. Cut it into eight pieces and lay them on a piece of double foil. Season well and scatter with the garlic and thyme leaves. Drizzle over 15ml/1 tbsp of the olive oil and a sprinkling of water. Bring the sides of the foil up to completely enclose the squash and secure the parcel.

3 Once the flames have died down, rake the hot coals to one side and insert a drip tray beside them. Fill the drip tray with water. Position a lightly oiled grill rack over the hot coals. Place the chicken on the grill rack above the drip tray, with the squash next to it, over the coals. Cover with a lid or tented heavy-duty foil. Cook the squash for 35 minutes, or until tender.

4 Drain the hickory chips and carefully add a handful to the coals, then replace the lid. Cook the chicken for 1–1¼ hours more, adding a handful of hickory chips every 15 minutes. Add the remaining rosemary to the coals with the last batch of hickory chips. When the chicken is done, transfer it to a plate, cover with tented foil and leave to stand for 10 minutes.

5 Unwrap the butternut squash. Leaving the thyme stalk behind, scoop the flesh and the garlic into a food processor. Pulse until the mixture forms a thick purée. Add the Parmesan, then the remaining oil, pulsing to ensure it is well combined. Spoon into a bowl and serve with the hot chicken. If the chicken is to be eaten cold, cover it once cool.

COOK'S TIP
With small barbecues, the coals may need to be replenished during cooking. Lift off the rack and chicken before the heat is too low and re-fuel. The coals will take about 10 minutes to heat sufficiently to continue. Allow for this when timing.

Energy 257kcal/1078kJ; Protein 34.4g; Carbohydrate 2.5g, of which sugars 1.9g; Fat 12.2g, of which saturates 2.7g; Cholesterol 98mg; Calcium 89mg; Fibre 1.1g; Sodium 126mg.

Skewered Poussins with Lime and Chilli

The poussins in this recipe are flattened out – spatchcocked – so that they will cook evenly and quickly. The breast is stuffed with chilli and sun-dried tomato butter, which keeps the meat moist and makes it taste wonderful.

SERVES FOUR

INGREDIENTS

4 poussins, about 450g/1lb each
40g/1¹/₂oz/3 tbsp butter
30ml/2 tbsp sun-dried tomato paste
finely grated rind of 1 lime
10ml/2 tsp chilli sauce
juice of ¹/₂ lime
flat leaf parsley sprigs, to garnish
lime wedges, to serve

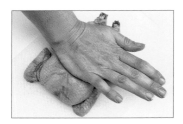

1 Place each poussin on a board, breast side up, and press down firmly with the palm of your hand, to break the breastbone.

2 Turn the poussin over and, with poultry shears or strong kitchen scissors, cut down either side of the backbone and remove it.

3 Turn the poussin breast side up and flatten it neatly. Lift the breast skin carefully and gently ease your fingertips underneath, to loosen it from the flesh.

4 Mix together the butter, sun-dried tomato paste, lime rind and chilli sauce. Spread about three-quarters of the mixture under the skin of the poussins, smoothing it evenly.

COOK'S TIP
If you wish to serve half a poussin per portion, use poultry shears or a large sharp knife to cut through the breastbone and then the backbone.

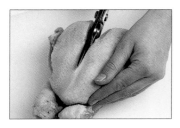

5 To hold the poussins flat during cooking, thread two skewers through each bird, crossing at the centre. Each skewer should pass through a wing and then out through a drumstick on the other side.

6 Prepare the barbecue. Position a lightly oiled grill rack over the hot coals. Mix the remaining tomato and butter mixture with the lime juice and brush it over the skin of the skewered poussins. Cook them over a medium-high heat, turning occasionally, for 25–30 minutes, or until the juices run clear when the thickest part of the leg is pierced. Garnish with flat leaf parsley and serve with lime wedges.

Energy 607kcal/2526kJ; Protein 50.4g; Carbohydrate 1.1g, of which sugars 1.1g; Fat 44.7g, of which saturates 15.1g; Cholesterol 282mg; Calcium 23mg; Fibre 0.2g; Sodium 259mg.

APRICOT DUCK <u>WITH</u> BEANSPROUTS

DUCK IS A RICHLY FLAVOURED BIRD AND IT GOES EXTREMELY WELL WHEN COOKED WITH FRUIT. HERE APRICOTS ARE USED TO STUFF DUCK BREASTS, WHICH ARE THEN BARBECUED WITH A HONEY GLAZE, MAKING DELICIOUSLY CRISPY SKIN ENCLOSING BEAUTIFULLY MOIST MEAT.

SERVES FOUR

INGREDIENTS
    4 plump duck breast portions
    1 small red onion, thinly sliced
    115g/4oz/½ cup ready-to-eat
        dried apricots
    15ml/1 tbsp clear honey
    5ml/1 tsp sesame oil
    10ml/2 tsp ground star anise
    salt and ground black pepper
For the salad
    ½ head Chinese leaves,
        finely shredded
    150g/5oz/2 cups beansprouts
    2 spring onions (scallions), shredded
    15ml/1 tbsp light soy sauce
    15ml/1 tbsp groundnut (peanut) oil
    5ml/1 tsp sesame oil
    5ml/1 tsp clear honey

1 Place the duck breast portions, skin side down, on a chopping board or clean work surface and cut a long slit down one side with a sharp kitchen knife, cutting not quite through, to form a large pocket.

2 Tuck the slices of onion and the apricots inside the pocket and press the breast firmly back into shape. Secure with metal skewers.

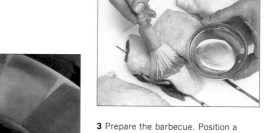

3 Prepare the barbecue. Position a lightly oiled grill rack over the hot coals. Mix together the clear honey and sesame oil, and brush generously over the duck, particularly the skin. Sprinkle over the star anise and season with plenty of salt and black pepper.

4 Cook the duck over medium-high heat for 12–15 minutes, turning once, until golden brown. The duck should be slightly pink in the centre.

5 Meanwhile, make the salad. Mix together the Chinese leaves, beansprouts and spring onions in a large bowl. Shake together the soy sauce, groundnut oil, sesame oil and honey in a screw-topped jar. Season to taste with salt and pepper.

6 Toss the salad with the dressing and serve with the duck.

Energy 338kcal/1420kJ; Protein 36.5g; Carbohydrate 19.7g, of which sugars 18.6g; Fat 16g, of which saturates 2.9g; Cholesterol 186mg; Calcium 79mg; Fibre 3.7g; Sodium 197mg.

RARE GINGERED DUCK

THIS IS JAPANESE AND CHINESE FUSION FOOD: THE TARE IS JAPANESE BUT THE PANCAKES ARE CHINESE. YOU CAN COOK THE DUCK USING A GRIDDLE OR DIRECTLY ON THE GRILL RACK OF THE BARBECUE. BOTH METHODS USE HIGH HEAT TO SEAR THE FLESH AND REMOVE THE FAT FOR SUCCULENT AND TASTY MEAT.

SERVES FOUR

INGREDIENTS

    4 large duck breast fillets, total
      weight about 675g/1½lb
    5cm/2in piece of fresh root ginger,
      finely grated
    ½ large cucumber
    12 Chinese pancakes
    6 spring onions (scallions),
      finely shredded

For the tare

    105ml/7 tbsp tamari
    105ml/7 tbsp mirin
    25g/1oz/2 tbsp sugar
    salt and ground black pepper

1 Make four slashes in the skin of each duck breast fillet, then lay them skin-side up on a plate. Squeeze the grated ginger over the duck to extract every drop of juice; discard the pulp. Generously rub the juice all over the duck, especially into the slashes. Using a vegetable peeler, peel the cucumber in strips, then cut it in half, scoop out the seeds and chop the flesh. Set aside in a bowl.

2 To make the tare, mix the tamari, mirin and sugar in a heavy pan and heat gently together until the sugar has dissolved. Increase the heat and simmer for 4–5 minutes, or until the syrup has reduced by about one-third.

3 Prepare the barbecue. Heat a griddle on the grill rack over hot coals. Sear the duck breasts in batches, placing them skin-side down.

4 When the fat has been rendered, and the skin is nicely browned, remove the duck from the pan. Drain off the fat and wipe the pan clean with kitchen paper. Reheat it, return the duck, flesh-side down and cook over a medium heat for about 3 minutes.

5 Brush on a little of the tare, turn the duck over, then, using a clean brush, brush the other side with tare and turn again. This should take about 1 minute, by which time the duck should be cooked rare. You can test for this by pressing the meat lightly: there should be some give in the flesh.

6 Remove from the pan and let the duck rest for a few minutes before slicing each breast across at an angle.

7 Warm the pancakes in a steamer for about 3 minutes. Serve with the duck, tare, spring onions and cucumber.

COOK'S TIP

To cook straight on the grill rack, part the hot coals in the centre and put a drip tray in the space. Position a lightly oiled grill rack over the hot coals. Sear the duck breasts directly over the coals, then move them over the drip tray. Cover with a lid or tented heavy-duty foil and cook as above, from step 4.

Energy 558kcal/2332kJ; Protein 36.4g; Carbohydrate 29.6g, of which sugars 7.6g; Fat 36.4g, of which saturates 6.1g; Cholesterol 186mg; Calcium 73mg; Fibre 1.2g; Sodium 293mg.

SPATCHCOCKED QUAIL <u>WITH</u> COUSCOUS

THESE DELICATE BABY BIRDS CAN BE COOKED VERY EFFICIENTLY ON A KETTLE BARBECUE WITH A LID.
IF YOUR BARBECUE DOESN'T HAVE ITS OWN LID, IMPROVISE WITH A LARGE UPTURNED WOK WITH A
WOODEN HANDLE OR USE TENTED FOIL. SERVE WITH A HERBY CHERRY TOMATO SALAD.

SERVES EIGHT

INGREDIENTS

8 quail
400ml/14fl oz/1⅔ cups water
2 lemons
60ml/4 tbsp extra virgin olive oil
45ml/3 tbsp chopped fresh
  tarragon leaves
125g/4¼oz/¾ cup couscous
15g/½oz dried (bell) peppers,
  finely chopped
8 black olives, pitted and chopped
salt and ground black pepper
16 wooden or metal skewers

1 Cut the backbones away from each quail and place them in a pan. Add the measured water and bring to the boil, then simmer gently to reduce the liquid by half. While the stock is cooking, wipe the insides of each bird with kitchen paper. If you find a heart inside, add it to the stock pot. Place each quail in turn, breast uppermost, on a board, and flatten it by pressing firmly on the breastbone. Carefully loosen the quail skin over the breasts with your fingers, creating a pocket for stuffing later.

COOK'S TIP

A lid is important for these fragile quail as it is best not to turn them. When enclosed, the heat circulates around the food, cooking it on all sides.

2 Grate the rind from the lemons. Set half the rind aside and put the rest in a flat dish. Squeeze both lemons and add the juice to the dish with 30ml/2 tbsp of the oil and 15ml/1 tbsp of the tarragon. Add the quail, turn to coat them well, cover and leave to marinate while you prepare the couscous stuffing.

3 Place the couscous in a medium bowl and add the dried peppers and salt and pepper. The stock should have reduced considerably by now. Strain 200ml/ 7fl oz/scant 1 cup over the couscous, cover with a dry cloth and leave to stand for 10 minutes.

4 Mix the reserved lemon rind into the couscous with the olives and the remaining tarragon and oil. Spread the mixture on a plate to cool, then cover and chill. When cold, ease a little stuffing into the breast pocket of each quail. If using wooden skewers, soak them in cold water for 30 minutes.

5 Prepare the barbecue. Pin the legs and wings of each quail to the body by driving a long skewer right through from either side to form a cross. If you want, wrap the leg tips with foil to prevent them from getting too charred.

6 Once the flames have died down, position a lightly oiled grill rack over the hot coals. Place the spatchcocked quail on the grill rack and cook over medium-high heat for about 5 minutes, moving the birds around occasionally. Cover with a lid or tented heavy-duty foil and cook for 10 minutes. Check if they are cooked; if they are plump and nicely browned they will almost certainly be done. If not, allow them to cook for a further 5 minutes. Let them stand for a few minutes to cool a little before serving, as they are best eaten with the fingers.

VEGETARIAN

*Barbecuing vegetables gives them a delicious flavour and they
can be combined with cheese, nuts, beans and tofu to make
some exciting main courses that will appeal to everyone.
The smoky flavours created by chargrilling really lift
vegetable fruits and roots such as aubergines, squashes,
peppers and asparagus, which can then be served with a
variety of dips and sauces. Halloumi cheese is a super
ingredient for the vegetarian barbecue because it has a firm
texture that does not melt in the same way as other cheeses
and so is useful to cook as an accompaniment to a melange of
grilled vegetables. You can also make rolls or parcels from the
vegetables themselves, such as sliced aubergines, and cook these
on the barbecue, as well as filling vegetables with aromatic
stuffings and cooking them over the coals or inside foil parcels.
With so many fantastic, flavourful combinations,
it's easy to plan a vegetarian barbecue feast.*

THAI VEGETABLE CAKES

HERE, NUTTY-TASTING TEMPEH, WHICH IS MADE FROM SOYBEANS, IS COMBINED WITH A FRAGRANT BLEND OF LEMON GRASS, FRESH CORIANDER AND GINGER, AND FORMED INTO SMALL PATTIES BEFORE BEING GRILLED. SERVE WITH THE DIPPING SAUCE, ACCOMPANIED BY A SWEET SAKE OR RICE WINE.

MAKES EIGHT

INGREDIENTS
1 lemon grass stalk, outer leaves
  removed and inside chopped
2 garlic cloves, chopped
2 spring onions (scallions), chopped
2 shallots, chopped
2 chillies, seeded and chopped
2.5cm/1in piece fresh root
  ginger, chopped
60ml/4 tbsp chopped fresh coriander
  (cilantro), plus extra to garnish
250g/9oz tempeh, thawed if
  frozen, sliced
15ml/1 tbsp lime juice

5ml/1 tsp sugar
45ml/3 tbsp plain (all-purpose) flour
1 large (US extra large) egg,
  lightly beaten
vegetable oil, for frying
salt and ground black pepper
For the dipping sauce
45ml/3 tbsp mirin
45ml/3 tbsp white wine vinegar
2 spring onions (scallions),
  thinly sliced
15ml/1 tbsp sugar
2 chillies, finely chopped
30ml/2 tbsp chopped fresh
  coriander (cilantro)
large pinch of salt

1 Prepare the barbecue. To make the dipping sauce, mix all the ingredients together in a small bowl and set aside.

2 Place the lemon grass, garlic, spring onions, shallots, chillies, ginger and coriander in a food processor or blender and process to a coarse paste. Add the tempeh, lime juice and sugar, then process to combine. Add the salt and pepper, flour and egg. Process again until the mixture forms a coarse, sticky paste. Position a lightly oiled grill rack over the hot coals.

3 Take one-eighth of the tempeh mixture at a time and form into balls with your hands – the mixture will be quite sticky, so it may help to dampen your palms. Gently flatten the balls.

4 Brush the tempeh cakes with oil. Cook over high heat for 5–6 minutes, turning once, until golden. Drain on kitchen paper. Garnish and serve warm with the dipping sauce.

Energy 119kcal/494kJ; Protein 4.5g; Carbohydrate 8.2g, of which sugars 3.6g; Fat 7.8g, of which saturates 1g; Cholesterol 24mg; Calcium 202mg; Fibre 1g; Sodium 15mg.

RED BEAN AND MUSHROOM BURGERS

*VEGETARIANS, VEGANS AND MEAT-EATERS ALIKE WILL ENJOY THESE HEALTHY, LOW-FAT VEGGIE BURGERS.
WITH SALAD, PITTA BREAD AND GREEK-STYLE YOGURT, THEY MAKE A SUBSTANTIAL MEAL. YOU MAY
FIND A HINGED WIRE GRILL USEFUL FOR COOKING THESE BURGERS.*

SERVES FOUR

INGREDIENTS
  15ml/1 tbsp olive oil
  1 small onion, finely chopped
  1 garlic clove, crushed
  5ml/1 tsp ground cumin
  5ml/1 tsp ground coriander
  2.5ml/½ tsp ground turmeric
  115g/4oz/1½ cups finely
    chopped mushrooms
  400g/14oz can red kidney beans
  30ml/2 tbsp chopped fresh
    coriander (cilantro)
  wholemeal (whole-wheat)
    flour (optional)
  olive oil, for brushing
  salt and ground black pepper
  Greek (US strained plain) yogurt,
    to serve

COOK'S TIP
Bean burgers are not quite as firm
as meat burgers, and will need careful
handling on the barbecue.

1 Heat the olive oil in a frying pan and
fry the onion and garlic over a medium
heat, stirring, until softened. Add the
spices and cook for a further minute,
stirring continuously.

2 Add the mushrooms and cook,
stirring, until softened and dry. Remove
the pan from the heat and empty the
contents into a large bowl.

3 Drain the red kidney beans
thoroughly, place them in a bowl and
mash them roughly with a fork.

4 Stir the kidney beans into the frying
pan, with the fresh coriander, and mix
thoroughly. Season the mixture well with
plenty of salt and pepper. Prepare the
barbecue. Position a lightly oiled grill
rack over the hot coals.

5 Using floured hands, form the mixture
into four flat burger shapes. If the
mixture is too sticky to handle, mix in a
little wholemeal flour.

6 Lightly brush the burgers with olive oil
and cook on a hot barbecue for
8–10 minutes, turning once, until
golden brown. Serve with a spoonful of
yogurt and a mixed salad, if you like.

Energy 159kcal/666kJ; Protein 7.6g; Carbohydrate 19.1g, of which sugars 4.5g; Fat 6.3g, of which saturates 0.9g; Cholesterol 0mg; Calcium 77mg; Fibre 6.7g; Sodium 392mg.

BARBECUED VEGETABLES WITH SMOKED TOMATO SALSA

USE A DOUBLE LAYER OF COALS TO START THE BARBECUE SO THAT THEY WILL BE DEEP ENOUGH TO MAKE A BED FOR THE FOIL-WRAPPED VEGETABLES, THEN GRILL THE TOMATOES ABOVE.

SERVES FOUR TO SIX

INGREDIENTS
  2 small whole heads of garlic
  2 butternut squash, about 450g/1lb
    each, halved lengthways and seeded
  4–6 onions, about 115g/4oz each,
    with a cross cut in the top of each
  4–6 baking potatoes, about
    175g/6oz each
  4–6 sweet potatoes, about
    175g/6oz each
  45ml/3 tbsp olive oil
  fresh thyme, bay leaf and
    rosemary sprigs
  salt and ground black pepper
  2 handfuls of hickory wood chips
    soaked in cold water for at least
    30 minutes
For the tomato salsa
  500g/1¼lb tomatoes, quartered
    and seeded
  2.5ml/½ tsp sugar
  a pinch of chilli flakes
  1.5ml/¼ tsp smoky sweet
    chilli powder
  30ml/2 tbsp good quality
    tomato chutney

1 Prepare a barbecue with plenty of coals. Wrap the garlic, squash and onions separately in a double layer of heavy-duty foil, leaving them open. Pair up the potatoes: one sweet, one ordinary. Drizzle a little oil over the contents of each packet, season well with salt and pepper and pop in a herb sprig. Spray with a little water and scrunch up the foil to secure the parcels.

2 Place the parcels on top of the coals heated to medium-high, noting what goes where, if possible. The garlic will take 20 minutes to cook, the squash 30 minutes, the onions 45 minutes and the potatoes 1 hour. As each vegetable cooks, remove the parcel and wrap it in an extra layer of foil to keep warm. Set aside. Shortly before serving, loosen the tops of all the parcels, except the garlic, and put them all back on the coals so that the vegetables dry out a little before being served.

3 Meanwhile, make the tomato salsa. Put a lightly oiled grill rack in place to heat. Sprinkle the tomatoes with sugar, chilli flakes and seasoning. Place them on the grill rack above the vegetables and cook, covered, for 5 minutes.

4 Drain the hickory chips and place a handful on the coals, replace the cover and leave to smoke for 5 minutes. Add some more wood chips and grill for 10 minutes more, or until the tomatoes have dried a little. Remove the tomatoes from the rack and spoon the flesh from the charred skins into a bowl, crush with a fork and mix in the other ingredients. Serve with the vegetables.

COOK'S TIP
The vegetables taste wonderful with grilled marinated sirloin steaks, or with Parmesan cheese shaved on top.

Energy 244kcal/1029kJ; Protein 6.2g; Carbohydrate 42.4g, of which sugars 13g; Fat 6.7g, of which saturates 1.1g; Cholesterol 0mg; Calcium 65mg; Fibre 5.4g; Sodium 54mg.

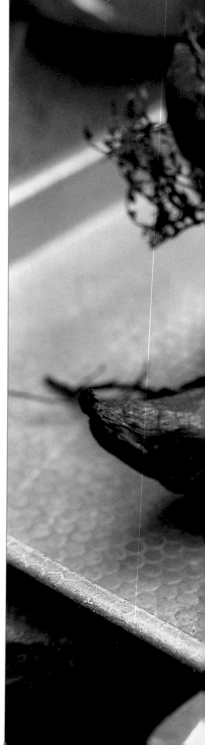

GRILLED VEGETABLES <u>WITH</u> SAFFRON DIP

A CREAMY DIP GOES VERY WELL WITH SIMPLY GRILLED VEGETABLES, AND HERE A DELICATELY FLAVOURED SAFFRON DIP IS SERVED WITH SLICED ROOT VEGETABLES AND ASPARAGUS SPEARS, MAKING AN UNUSUAL COMBINATION. SLICING THE VEGETABLES MEANS THAT THEY COOK MORE QUICKLY.

SERVES FOUR TO SIX

INGREDIENTS
    4 small sweet potatoes, total weight
        about 675g/1½lb
    4 carrots, total weight about
        375g/13oz
    parsnips, total weight about
        400g/14oz
    4 raw beetroot (beets), total weight
        about 400g/14oz
    450g/1lb asparagus, trimmed
    60ml/4 tbsp extra virgin olive oil
    salt and ground black pepper
For the saffron dip
    15ml/1 tbsp boiling water
    small pinch of saffron threads
    200ml/7fl oz/scant 1 cup fromage
        frais or crème fraîche
    10 fresh chives, chopped
    10 fresh basil leaves, torn

1 To make the saffron dip, pour the measured boiling water into a small bowl and add the saffron strands. Leave to infuse for 3 minutes. Beat the fromage frais or crème fraîche until smooth, then stir in the infused saffron liquid.

2 Add the chopped chives and basil leaves. Season and stir to combine. Transfer to a serving bowl.

3 Prepare the barbecue. Cutting lengthways, slice each sweet potato and carrot into 8 pieces, each parsnip into 7 and each beetroot into 10. Toss all the vegetables except the beetroot in most of the oil in a large tray. Put the beetroot on a separate tray, because it might otherwise bleed over all the other vegetables. Gently toss the beetroot in the remaining oil and season all the vegetables well.

4 Position a lightly oiled grill rack over the hot coals. Arrange the vegetables on the grill rack over medium heat.

5 Lightly grill the vegetables for 3 minutes on each side, or until tender and branded with grill lines. Remove them as they cook and serve hot or warm with the saffron dip.

Energy 397kcal/1660kJ; Protein 7g; Carbohydrate 44.6g, of which sugars 21.6g; Fat 22.4g, of which saturates 10.5g; Cholesterol 38mg; Calcium 123mg; Fibre 9.8g; Sodium 119mg.

MOROCCAN-STYLE CHARGRILLED VEGETABLES

CHARGRILLED VEGETABLES ARE GIVEN EXTRA FLAVOUR BY ADDING GARLIC, GINGER, ROSEMARY AND HONEY, AND TASTE DELICIOUS WITH COUSCOUS. YOGURT OR HARISSA GO VERY WELL WITH THE DISH. SERVE WITH A SALAD OF MOZZARELLA TOSSED WITH DRESSED SALAD LEAVES.

SERVES SIX

INGREDIENTS
  75ml/5 tbsp olive oil
  6 garlic cloves, crushed
  25g/1oz fresh root ginger, grated
  a few large fresh rosemary sprigs
  10ml/2 tsp clear honey
  3 red onions, peeled and quartered
  2–3 courgettes (zucchini), halved
    lengthways and cut across into
    2–3 pieces
  2–3 red, green or yellow (bell)
    peppers, seeded and quartered
  2 aubergines (eggplants), cut into
    6–8 long segments
  2–3 leeks, trimmed and cut into
    long strips
  2–3 sweet potatoes, peeled,
    halved lengthways and cut
    into long strips
  4–6 tomatoes, quartered
  salt and ground black pepper
  natural (plain) yogurt or harissa,
    to serve
For the couscous
  500g/1¼lb/2¾ cups couscous
  5ml/1 tsp salt
  600ml/1 pint/2½ cups warm water
  45ml/3 tbsp sunflower oil
  about 25g/1oz/2 tbsp butter, diced

1 Preheat the oven to 200°C/400°F/ Gas 6. Put the couscous in a bowl. Stir the salt into the water, then pour it over the couscous, stirring to make sure it is absorbed evenly. Leave to stand for 10 minutes to plump up then, using your fingers, rub the sunflower oil into the grains to air them and break up any lumps. Tip the couscous into an ovenproof dish, arrange the butter over the top, cover with foil and heat in the oven for about 20 minutes.

2 Meanwhile, prepare the barbecue. Position a lightly oiled grill rack over the hot coals and heat a griddle on the grill rack.

3 Pour the oil into a large baking tray and add the garlic, ginger, rosemary and honey. Season with salt and pepper. Toss the vegetables in the flavoured oil to coat evenly. Cook the larger pieces of vegetables directly on the grill rack over medium-high heat and the smaller pieces, such as the tomatoes and onions, on the griddle, brushing with oil as required. As the vegetables cook, transfer them to a dish, cover and keep warm.

4 To serve, use your fingers to work the melted butter into the grains of couscous and fluff it up, then pile it on a large dish and shape into a mound with a little pit at the top. Spoon some vegetables into the pit and arrange the rest around the dish. Serve immediately with yogurt, or harissa if you prefer.

Energy 337kcal/1416kJ; Protein 11.5g; Carbohydrate 43.5g, of which sugars 7.1g; Fat 14.2g, of which saturates 5.9g; Cholesterol 23mg; Calcium 206mg; Fibre 5.3g; Sodium 613mg.

GRIDDLED HALLOUMI AND BEAN SALAD

HALLOUMI IS THAT HARD, WHITE, SALTY GOAT'S MILK CHEESE THAT SQUEAKS WHEN YOU BITE IT. IT GRILLS REALLY WELL AND IS THE PERFECT COMPLEMENT TO THE LOVELY FRESH-TASTING FLAVOURS OF THE VEGETABLES. THIS SALAD CAN BE GRILLED DIRECTLY ON THE GRILL RACK OVER MEDIUM HEAT.

SERVES FOUR

INGREDIENTS

- 20 baby new potatoes, total weight about 300g/11oz
- 200g/7oz extra-fine green beans, trimmed
- 675g/1½lb broad (fava) beans, shelled (shelled weight about 225g/8oz)
- 200g/7oz halloumi cheese, cut into 5mm/¼in slices
- 1 garlic clove, crushed to a paste with a large pinch of salt
- 90ml/6 tbsp olive oil
- 5ml/1 tsp cider vinegar or white wine vinegar
- 15g/½oz/½ cup fresh basil leaves, shredded
- 45ml/3 tbsp chopped fresh savory
- 2 spring onions (scallions), finely sliced
- salt and ground black pepper
- 4 metal or wooden skewers

1 Thread five potatoes on to each skewer, and cook in a large pan of salted boiling water for about 7 minutes, or until almost tender. Add the green beans and cook for 3 minutes more. Tip in the broad beans and cook for just 2 minutes. Drain all the vegetables in a large colander.

2 Remove the potatoes, still on their skewers, from the colander, then refresh the cooked broad beans under plenty of cold running water. Pop each broad bean out of its skin to reveal the bright green inner bean. Place the beans in a bowl, cover and set aside.

3 Place the halloumi slices and the potato skewers in a wide dish. Whisk the garlic and oil together with a generous grinding of black pepper. Add to the dish and toss the halloumi and potato skewers until they are coated in the mixture.

4 Prepare the barbecue and rake the hot coals to one side. Place the cheese and potato skewers in the griddle and cook over the coals for about 2 minutes on each side. If they over-char, move the griddle to the cooler side of the grill rack.

5 Add the vinegar to the oil and garlic remaining in the dish and whisk to mix. Toss in the broad beans, herbs and spring onions, with the cooked halloumi. Serve, with the potato skewers laid alongside.

Energy 238kcal/996kJ; Protein 14.7g; Carbohydrate 21.3g, of which sugars 3.9g; Fat 11g, of which saturates 7g; Cholesterol 35mg; Calcium 244mg; Fibre 5.8g; Sodium 735mg.

GRILLED FENNEL SALAD

THIS IS SO TYPICALLY ITALIAN THAT IF YOU CLOSE YOUR EYES YOU COULD BE ON A TUSCAN HILLSIDE,
SITTING UNDER A SHADY TREE AND ENJOYING AN ELEGANT LUNCH. FENNEL HAS MANY FANS, BUT IS
OFTEN USED RAW OR LIGHTLY BRAISED, MAKING THIS GRIDDLE RECIPE A DELIGHTFUL DISCOVERY.

SERVES SIX

INGREDIENTS

3 sweet baby orange (bell) peppers
5 fennel bulbs with green tops, total
   weight about 900g/2lb
30ml/2 tbsp olive oil
15ml/1 tbsp cider or white wine
   vinegar
45ml/3 tbsp extra virgin olive oil
24 small niçoise olives
2 long sprigs of fresh savory, leaves
   removed
salt and ground black pepper

COOK'S TIP
If cooking directly on the barbecue, char
the peppers when the coals are hot, then
cool them ready for peeling. Grill the
fennel over medium-hot coals and turn
frequently once stripes have formed.

1 Prepare the barbecue. Heat a griddle
on the grill rack over hot coals. Roast
the baby peppers, turning them every
few minutes until charred all over.
Remove the pan from the heat, place
the peppers under an upturned bowl
and leave to cool a little and for the
skins to loosen.

2 Remove the green fronds from the
fennel and reserve. Slice the fennel
lengthways into five roughly equal
pieces. If the root looks a little tough,
cut it out.

3 Place the fennel pieces in a flat dish,
coat with the olive oil and season. Rub
off the charred skin from the grilled
peppers – it should come away easily –
remove the seeds and cut the flesh
into small dice.

4 Re-heat the griddle and test the
temperature again, then lower the heat
slightly and grill the fennel slices in
batches for about 8–10 minutes, turning
frequently, until they are branded with
golden grill marks. Monitor the heat so
they cook through without over-charring.
As each batch cooks, transfer it to a flat
serving dish.

5 Whisk the vinegar and olive oil
together until thoroughly combined,
then pour the dressing over the fennel.
Gently fold in the diced baby orange
peppers and the niçoise olives. Tear
the savory leaves and fennel fronds
and scatter them over the salad. Serve
either warm or cold.

Energy 96kcal/397kJ; Protein 2.5g; Carbohydrate 9.1g, of which sugars 8.7g; Fat 5.7g, of which saturates 0.8g; Cholesterol 0mg; Calcium 52mg; Fibre 5.6g; Sodium 302mg.

CARROT AND ORANGE SALAD

THIS IS A WONDERFUL, FRESH-TASTING SALAD WITH SUCH A FABULOUS COMBINATION OF CITRUS FRUIT AND VEGETABLES THAT IT IS DIFFICULT TO KNOW WHETHER IT IS A SALAD OR A DESSERT. IT MAKES A REFRESHING ACCOMPANIMENT TO GRILLED MEAT, CHICKEN OR FISH.

SERVES FOUR

INGREDIENTS
450g/1lb carrots
2 large navel oranges
15ml/1 tbsp extra virgin olive oil
30ml/2 tbsp freshly squeezed
  lemon juice
pinch of sugar (optional)
30ml/2 tbsp chopped pistachio nuts
  or toasted pine nuts
salt and ground black pepper

1 Peel the carrots and coarsely grate them into a large bowl.

2 Cut a thin slice of peel and pith from each end of the oranges. Place cut-side down on a plate and cut off the peel and pith in strips. Holding the oranges over a bowl and using a sharp knife, carefully cut out each segment leaving the membrane behind. Squeeze the juice from the membrane into the bowl.

3 Blend the oil, lemon juice and orange juice in a small bowl to make a light dressing. Season with salt and freshly ground black pepper, and a little sugar, if you like.

4 Toss the oranges with the carrots and pour the dressing over. Sprinkle over the pistachios or pine nuts and serve.

Energy 131kcal/547kJ; Protein 2.7g; Carbohydrate 14.6g, of which sugars 13.9g; Fat 7.3g, of which saturates 1.1g; Cholesterol 0mg; Calcium 65mg; Fibre 4.2g; Sodium 71mg.

TABBOULEH

THIS IS A WONDERFULLY REFRESHING, TANGY SALAD OF SOAKED BULGUR WHEAT AND MASSES OF FRESH MINT, PARSLEY AND SPRING ONIONS. FEEL FREE TO INCREASE THE AMOUNT OF HERBS FOR A GREENER SALAD. IT CAN BE SERVED AS AN APPETIZER OR AS AN ACCOMPANIMENT TO A MAIN COURSE.

SERVES FOUR TO SIX

INGREDIENTS
250g/9oz/1½ cups bulgur wheat
1 large bunch spring onions
  (scallions), thinly sliced
1 cucumber, finely chopped or diced
3 tomatoes, chopped
1.5–2.5ml/¼–½ tsp ground cumin
1 large bunch fresh parsley, chopped
1 large bunch fresh mint, chopped
juice of 2 lemons, or to taste
60ml/4 tbsp extra virgin olive oil
salt
olives, lemon wedges, tomato wedges,
  cucumber slices and mint sprigs,
  to garnish (optional)
cos or romaine lettuce and natural
  (plain) yogurt, to serve (optional)

1 Pick over the bulgur wheat to remove any dirt. Place it in a bowl, cover with cold water and leave to soak for about 30 minutes.

2 Tip the bulgur wheat into a sieve and drain well, shaking to remove any excess water, then return it to the bowl.

3 Add the spring onions to the bulgur wheat, then mix and squeeze together with your hands to combine.

4 Add the cucumber, tomatoes, cumin, parsley, mint, lemon juice, oil and salt to the bulgur wheat and toss to combine.

5 Heap the tabbouleh on to a bed of lettuce and garnish with olives, lemon and tomato wedges, cucumber and mint sprigs and serve with a bowl of natural yogurt, if you like.

VARIATIONS
Use couscous soaked in boiling water in place of the bulgur wheat and use chopped fresh coriander (cilantro) instead of parsley.

Energy 180kcal/748kJ; Protein 3.6g; Carbohydrate 24.3g, of which sugars 2.8g; Fat 8.1g, of which saturates 1.1g; Cholesterol 0mg; Calcium 42mg; Fibre 1.4g; Sodium 10mg.

AUBERGINE AND BUTTERNUT SALAD

BEAUTIFULLY GOLDEN BUTTERNUT SQUASH MAKES A SUBSTANTIAL SALAD WITH GRIDDLED AUBERGINE AND FETA CHEESE. LIKE ALL RECIPES FOR GRIDDLED FOOD, THIS SALAD CAN BE COOKED INDOORS AT ANY TIME OF THE YEAR AND IS JUST AS DELICIOUS IN THE WINTER AS IN THE SUMMER.

SERVES FOUR

INGREDIENTS
2 aubergines (eggplants)
1 butternut squash, about 1kg/2¼lb, peeled
120ml/4fl oz/½ cup extra virgin olive oil
5ml/1 tsp paprika
150g/5oz feta cheese
50g/2oz/⅓ cup pistachio nuts, roughly chopped
salt and ground black pepper

1 Slice the aubergines widthways into 5mm/¼in rounds. Spread them out on a tray and sprinkle with a little salt. Leave for 30 minutes. Slice the squash in the same way, scooping out any seeds with a spoon. Place the butternut squash slices in a bowl, season lightly and toss with 30ml/2 tbsp of the oil.

2 Prepare the barbecue. Heat a griddle on the grill rack over hot coals. Lower the heat a little and grill the butternut squash slices in batches. Sear for about 3 minutes on each side, then put them on a tray. Continue until all the slices have been cooked, then dust with a little of the paprika.

3 Pat the aubergine slices dry. Toss with the remaining oil and season lightly. Cook in the same way as the squash. When all the slices are cooked, mix the aubergine and squash together in a bowl. Crumble the feta cheese over the warm salad, scatter the pistachio nuts over the top and dust with the remaining paprika.

VARIATION
Instead of aubergines try (bell) peppers or thinly sliced courgettes (zucchini) or add a few small onions or quartered onions with the root attached. Add a few raisins as well, if you like.

Energy 393kcal/1626kJ; Protein 11.2g; Carbohydrate 10.4g, of which sugars 8.5g; Fat 34.3g, of which saturates 9.2g; Cholesterol 26mg; Calcium 236mg; Fibre 6.3g; Sodium 609mg.

AUBERGINE ROLLS IN TOMATO SAUCE

THIS IS A USEFUL AND TASTY VEGETARIAN DISH THAT CAN BE PREPARED IN ADVANCE AND SIMPLY FINISHED OVER THE BARBECUE. LITTLE AUBERGINE ROLLS CONTAIN A FILLING OF RICOTTA AND GOAT'S CHEESE WITH RICE, FLAVOURED WITH BASIL AND MINT, AND THEY GO VERY WELL WITH A TOMATO SAUCE.

<u>SERVES FOUR</u>

INGREDIENTS
  2 aubergines (eggplants)
  olive oil, or sunflower oil for
    shallow frying
  75g/3oz/scant ½ cup ricotta cheese
  75g/3oz/scant ½ cup soft
    goat's cheese
  225g/8oz/2 cups cooked long
    grain rice
  15ml/1 tbsp chopped fresh basil
  5ml/1 tsp chopped fresh mint, plus
    mint sprigs, to garnish
  salt and ground black pepper
For the tomato sauce
  15ml/1 tbsp olive oil
  1 red onion, finely chopped
  1 garlic clove, crushed
  400g/14oz can chopped tomatoes
  120ml/4fl oz/½ cup vegetable stock
    or white wine, or a mixture
  15ml/1 tbsp chopped fresh parsley

COOK'S TIP
If you would prefer to use less oil for
the aubergines, brush each slice with
just a little oil, then barbecue until
evenly browned.

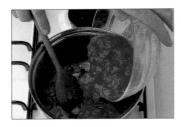

1 To make the tomato sauce, heat the oil in a small pan and fry the onion and garlic for 3–4 minutes until softened. Add the tomatoes, vegetable stock and/or wine, and parsley. Season well. Bring to the boil, then lower the heat and simmer for 10–12 minutes, or until slightly thickened, stirring.

2 Cut each aubergine into 4–5 slices, discarding the two outer slices, which consist largely of skin. Heat the oil in a large frying pan and fry the aubergine slices until they are golden brown on both sides. Drain on kitchen paper. Mix the ricotta, goat's cheese, rice, basil and mint in a bowl. Season well with salt and pepper.

3 Prepare the barbecue. Position a lightly oiled grill rack over the hot coals. Place a generous spoonful of the cheese and rice mixture at one end of each aubergine slice and roll up. Wrap the aubergine rolls in four foil parcels and place on the grill rack. Cook for 15 minutes over medium heat. Reheat the tomato sauce on the barbecue until thoroughly bubbling. Garnish with the mint sprigs and serve with the sauce.

Energy 233kcal/980kJ; Protein 8.9g; Carbohydrate 24.6g, of which sugars 6.7g; Fat 11.8g, of which saturates 5.8g; Cholesterol 25mg; Calcium 56mg; Fibre 3.3g; Sodium 125mg.

TOFU AND PEPPER KEBABS

A CRUNCHY COATING OF GROUND, DRY-ROASTED PEANUTS PRESSED ON TO CUBED TOFU PROVIDES PLENTY OF ADDITIONAL TEXTURE AND COLOUR. ALONG WITH THE CHARGRILLED, SUCCULENT CHUNKS OF RED AND GREEN PEPPERS, THESE SIMPLE ADDITIONS GIVE THE KEBABS A SUBTLE FLAVOUR.

SERVES TWO

INGREDIENTS
    250g/9oz firm tofu
    50g/2oz/½ cup dry-roasted peanuts
    45ml/3 tbsp olive oil
    2 red and 2 green (bell) peppers
    60ml/4 tbsp sweet chilli
      dipping sauce
    salt and ground black pepper

1 Soak four long wooden skewers in water for 30 minutes. Pat the tofu dry on kitchen paper and then cut it into small cubes.

2 Grind the peanuts in a blender or food processor and transfer to a plate. Put the oil in a bowl and add the tofu cubes. Toss in the oil until well coated. Lift the tofu cubes out of the oil and turn them in the ground nuts to coat.

3 Prepare the barbecue. Position a lightly oiled grill rack over the hot coals. Halve and seed the peppers, and cut them into large chunks.

4 Brush the chunks of pepper with the oil from the bowl and thread them on to the skewers, alternating with the tofu cubes. Season with salt and pepper. Place on the grill rack.

5 Cook the kebabs over medium heat, turning frequently, for 10–12 minutes, or until the peppers and peanuts are beginning to brown. Transfer the kebabs to warmed plates and serve immediately with the dipping sauce.

COOK'S TIP
Chilli sauces vary from fairly mild to searingly hot, while some are quite sweet. The hot ones go particularly well with these kebabs.

Energy 516kcal/2143kJ; Protein 20.3g; Carbohydrate 30.2g, of which sugars 26.8g; Fat 35.6g, of which saturates 5.6g; Cholesterol 0mg; Calcium 681mg; Fibre 7.4g; Sodium 461mg.

STUFFED PEPPERS

ALMONDS, DRIED FRUIT, RICE AND GARLIC MAKE A RICH AND TASTY FILLING FOR PEPPERS, WHICH CAN BE COOKED IN FOIL PARCELS ON THE GRILL RACK. PREPARE THEM JUST AS YOU ARE READY TO COOK THEM SO THAT THE FILLING IS STILL HOT WHEN THE PEPPERS GO ON THE BARBECUE.

SERVES FOUR

INGREDIENTS
    1 ripe tomato, peeled
    2 yellow or orange and 2 green
      (bell) peppers
    60ml/4 tbsp olive oil, plus extra
      for sprinkling
    2 onions, chopped
    2 garlic cloves, crushed
    75g/3oz/½ cup blanched
      almonds, chopped
    75g/3oz/scant ½ cup long grain rice,
      boiled and drained
    30ml/2 tbsp fresh mint,
      roughly chopped
    30ml/2 tbsp fresh parsley,
      roughly chopped
    30ml/2 tbsp sultanas (golden raisins)
    45ml/3 tbsp ground almonds
    salt and ground black pepper
    chopped mixed fresh herbs,
      to garnish

1 Prepare the barbecue. Position a grill rack over the hot coals. Roughly chop the tomato and set it aside.

2 Halve the peppers, leaving the cores intact. Scoop out the seeds. Brush the peppers with 15ml/1 tbsp of the olive oil and cook over a medium heat for 15 minutes. Place each pair of peppers on a piece of double-thickness foil and season well with salt and pepper.

3 Fry the onions in the remaining olive oil for 5 minutes. Add the garlic and almonds to the pan and fry for a further minute.

4 Remove the pan from the heat and stir in the rice, tomato, mint, parsley and sultanas. Season well with salt and pepper and spoon the mixture into the peppers.

5 Scatter with the ground almonds and sprinkle with a little extra olive oil. Wrap the peppers in the foil and place on the grill rack. Cook over medium-high heat for 20–25 minutes. Serve garnished with fresh herbs.

VARIATION
Add a few stuffed tomatoes to the recipe to complement the peppers. Simply halve and scoop out the seeds and pulp; reserve the latter to add to the stuffing.

Energy 392kcal/1630kJ; Protein 9.2g; Carbohydrate 25.4g, of which sugars 17.9g; Fat 28.8g, of which saturates 3.2g; Cholesterol 0mg; Calcium 110mg; Fibre 5.5g; Sodium 19mg.

STUFFED ARTICHOKE HALVES

*THE DISTINCTIVE FLAVOUR OF GLOBE ARTICHOKES IS ACCENTUATED WHEN THEY ARE CHARGRILLED,
AND IN THIS RECIPE THEY ARE TOPPED WITH AN INTENSELY SAVOURY STUFFING OF MUSHROOMS,
GRUYÈRE CHEESE AND WALNUTS, MAKING THEM RICH AND FLAVOURSOME.*

SERVES FOUR

INGREDIENTS
225g/8oz/3 cups mushrooms
15g/½oz/1 tbsp butter
2 shallots, finely chopped
50g/2oz/¼ cup full- or medium-fat
  soft cheese
30ml/2 tbsp chopped walnuts
45ml/3 tbsp grated Gruyère cheese
4 large or 6 small artichoke bottoms
  (from cooked artichokes, leaves and
  choke removed, or cooked frozen or
  canned artichoke hearts)
salt and ground black pepper
fresh parsley sprigs, to garnish

1 To make the duxelles for the stuffing,
put the mushrooms in a food processor
or blender and pulse until they are
finely chopped.

2 Melt the butter in a frying pan and
cook the shallots over a medium heat
for about 2–3 minutes, or until just
softened. Add the mushrooms, raise the
heat slightly, and cook for 5–7 minutes
more, stirring frequently, until all the
liquid from the mushrooms has been
driven off and they are almost dry.
Season with plenty of salt and freshly
ground black pepper. Position a lightly
oiled grill rack over the hot coals.

3 In a large bowl, combine the soft
cheese and cooked mushrooms. Add
the walnuts and half the Gruyère
cheese, and stir well to combine
the mixture.

4 Divide the mixture among the
artichoke bottoms and sprinkle over the
remaining cheese. Cook over medium
heat for 12 minutes covered with a lid
or tented foil. Garnish and serve.

COOK'S TIP
To cook fresh artichokes, trim the stalk
and boil for 40–45 minutes. Trim away
the leaves down to the base. Scrape
away the hairy choke.

Energy 162kcal/672kJ; Protein 6.4g; Carbohydrate 2.2g, of which sugars 1.7g; Fat 14.1g, of which saturates 6g; Cholesterol 24mg; Calcium 103mg; Fibre 1.2g; Sodium 115mg.

BEAN- AND LEMON-STUFFED MUSHROOMS

LARGE FIELD MUSHROOMS HAVE A RICH FLAVOUR AND A MEATY TEXTURE THAT GO WELL WITH THIS FRAGRANT HERB, BEAN AND LEMON STUFFING. THE GARLIC AND PINE NUT ACCOMPANIMENT IS A TRADITIONAL MIDDLE EASTERN DISH WITH A SMOOTH, CREAMY CONSISTENCY.

SERVES FOUR

INGREDIENTS
  200g/7oz/1 cup dried or 400g/14oz/
    2 cups drained, canned aduki beans
  45ml/3 tbsp olive oil, plus extra
    for brushing
  1 onion, finely chopped
  2 garlic cloves, crushed
  30ml/2 tbsp fresh chopped or 5ml/
    1 tsp dried thyme
  8 large field (portobello) mushrooms,
    stalks finely chopped
  50g/2oz/1 cup fresh wholemeal
    (whole-wheat) breadcrumbs
  juice of 1 lemon
  185g/6½oz/generous ¾ cup
    crumbled goat's cheese
  salt and ground black pepper
For the pine nut paste
  50g/2oz/½ cup pine nuts,
    lightly toasted
  50g/2oz/1 cup cubed white bread
  2 garlic cloves, chopped
  about 200ml/7fl oz/scant 1 cup milk
  45ml/3 tbsp olive oil
  15ml/1 tbsp chopped fresh parsley,
    to garnish (optional)

1 If using dried beans, soak them overnight, then drain and rinse well. Place in a pan, add enough water to cover and bring to the boil. Boil rapidly for 10 minutes, then reduce the heat, cook for 30 minutes, or until tender, then drain. If using canned beans, drain, rinse under cold running water, then drain well again, and set aside.

2 Heat the oil in a large, heavy frying pan, add the onion and garlic and cook over a low heat, stirring frequently, for 5 minutes, or until softened.

3 Add the thyme and the mushroom stalks and cook for a further 3 minutes, stirring occasionally, until tender.

4 Stir in the aduki beans, breadcrumbs and lemon juice, season to taste then cook gently for 2–3 minutes, or until heated through. Mash about two-thirds of the beans with a fork or potato masher, leaving the remaining beans whole, then mix thoroughly together. Prepare the barbecue. Position a lightly oiled grill rack over the hot coals.

5 To make the pine nut paste, place all the ingredients in a food processor or blender and process until smooth and creamy. Add a little more milk if the mixture appears too thick. Sprinkle with parsley, if using.

6 Brush the base and sides of the mushrooms with oil. Top each with a spoonful of the bean mixture. Cook over medium heat for 20 minutes covered with a lid or tented heavy-duty foil.

7 Top each mushroom with cheese and grill for 5 minutes more, or until the cheese is melted. Serve with a green leaf salad, if you like, or wilted spinach.

Energy 604kcal/2520kJ; Protein 25.5g; Carbohydrate 38.8g, of which sugars 8.7g; Fat 39.7g, of which saturates 12g; Cholesterol 46mg; Calcium 237mg; Fibre 8.8g; Sodium 858mg.

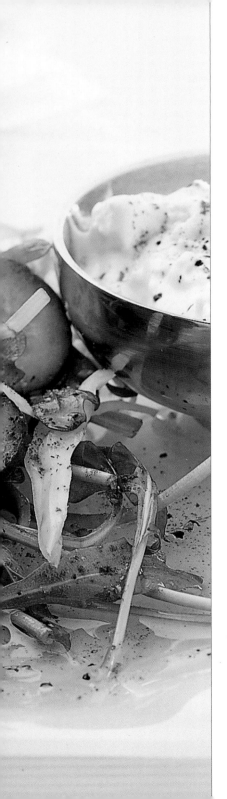

SIDE DISHES AND ACCOMPANIMENTS

Many of the side dishes for barbecued main dishes can be cooked on (or even in) the barbecue itself. Vegetables can be simply roasted wrapped in foil nestling between the coals while you grill the main course on the grill rack above. Serve them with a spicy dip or a richly flavoured butter and you will have side dishes that taste just as exciting as the main dish. You can also grill vegetables directly on the grill rack and they will have that wonderful smoky flavour — try buttery Husk-grilled Corn on the Cob or Grilled Potatoes with Chive Flowers. Probably the most useful side dishes are the salads that you can prepare in advance and bring out while everything is cooking. This chapter also includes cold salads that will contrast well with your barbecued meat, fish, poultry or vegetarian feast: refreshing and crisp or deliciously creamy — side orders to tempt every palate.

CHARGRILLED AUBERGINE AND LEMON SALAD

LEMON SUBTLY UNDERLINES THE FLAVOUR OF MELTINGLY SOFT AUBERGINE IN THIS CLASSIC SICILIAN DISH. IT IS DELICIOUS SERVED AS AN ACCOMPANIMENT TO A PLATTER OF COLD MEATS, WITH PASTA OR SIMPLY ON ITS OWN WITH SOME GOOD CRUSTY BREAD.

SERVES FOUR

INGREDIENTS

   1 large aubergine (eggplant),
      about 675g/1½lb
   60ml/4 tbsp olive oil
   grated rind and juice of 1 lemon
   30ml/2 tbsp capers, rinsed
   12 pitted green olives
   30ml/2 tbsp chopped fresh flat
      leaf parsley
   salt and ground black pepper

COOK'S TIP

This salad will taste even better when made the day before. It will keep well, covered in the refrigerator, for up to 4 days. Return the salad to room temperature before serving.

1 Prepare the barbecue. Heat a griddle on the grill rack over the hot coals. Cut the aubergine into 2.5cm/1in cubes. Place in a bowl and pour in the oil. Toss well so that the cubes are well coated. Griddle the aubergine cubes in batches over medium heat for about 10 minutes, tossing frequently, until golden and softened. Remove with a slotted spoon, drain on kitchen paper and sprinkle with a little salt.

2 Place the aubergine cubes in a large serving bowl, toss with the lemon rind and juice, capers, olives and chopped parsley, and season well with salt and pepper. Serve at room temperature.

VARIATION

Add toasted pine nuts and shavings of Parmesan cheese for a main course dish.

Energy 140kcal/580kJ; Protein 1.9g; Carbohydrate 4g, of which sugars 3.6g; Fat 13.2g, of which saturates 2g; Cholesterol 0mg; Calcium 42mg; Fibre 4.2g; Sodium 288mg.

STUFFED VEGETABLE CUPS

THE SPICY, TOMATO-RED FILLING OF THESE VEGETABLES CARRIES AN IRRESISTABLY TART CITRUS TANG. THESE VERSATILE VEGETARIAN TREATS ARE EQUALLY DELICIOUS HOT OR COLD AND ARE IDEAL SERVED AS AN APPETIZER OR AS A LIGHT MAIN COURSE.

SERVES FOUR

INGREDIENTS

4 potatoes, peeled
4 onions, skinned
4 courgettes (zucchini),
  halved widthways
2–4 garlic cloves, chopped
45–60ml/3–4 tbsp olive oil
45–60ml/3–4 tbsp tomato
  purée (paste)
1.5ml/¼ tsp ras al hanout or
  curry powder
large pinch of ground allspice
seeds of 2–3 cardamom pods
juice of ½ lemon
30–45ml/2–3 tbsp chopped
  fresh parsley
90–120ml/6–8 tbsp vegetable stock
salt and ground black pepper
salad, to serve (optional)

1 Bring a large pan of salted water to the boil. Starting with the potatoes, then the onions and finally the courgettes, add to the boiling water and cook until they become almost tender but not cooked through. Allow about 10 minutes for the potatoes, 8 minutes for the onions and 4–6 minutes for the courgettes. Remove the vegetables from the pan and leave to cool.

COOK'S TIP
If possible, use a small melon baller or apple corer to hollow out the vegetables. It will be much easier and neater than using a teaspoon.

2 When the vegetables are cool enough to handle, hollow them out, retaining the flesh. Prepare the barbecue. Position a grill rack over the hot coals.

3 Finely chop the scooped-out vegetable flesh and put in a bowl. Add the garlic, half the olive oil, the tomato purée, ras al hanout or curry powder, allspice, cardamom seeds, lemon juice, parsley and salt and pepper, and mix well together. Use the stuffing mixture to fill the hollowed out vegetables.

4 Place each vegetable in a double thickness of foil and drizzle with the stock and the remaining oil. Wrap the foil tightly around the vegetables. Cook over medium-high heat for 35–40 minutes or until tender. Serve warm with a salad, if you like.

Energy 225kcal/937kJ; Protein 6.4g; Carbohydrate 30.2g, of which sugars 12.3g; Fat 9.5g, of which saturates 1.4g; Cholesterol 0mg; Calcium 98mg; Fibre 4.8g; Sodium 47mg.

GRILLED POTATOES WITH CHIVE FLOWERS

THERE IS SOMETHING VERY ENJOYABLE ABOUT USING EDIBLE FLOWERING PLANTS AND HERBS FROM THE GARDEN. GRABBING A HANDFUL OF THIS HERB OR THAT FLOWER IS ALL PART OF THE CREATIVITY OF COOKING AND EATING OUTDOORS, AND IT CAN PRODUCE REALLY EXCITING AND UNEXPECTED RESULTS.

SERVES FOUR TO SIX

INGREDIENTS
    900g/2lb salad potatoes, such as
      charlottes, Jersey royals or
      French ratte
    15ml/1 tbsp champagne vinegar
    105ml/7 tbsp olive oil
    45ml/3 tbsp chopped chives
    about 10 chive flowers
    4–6 small bunches yellow cherry
      tomatoes on the vine
    salt and ground black pepper

COOK'S TIP
If well established in the garden, chives
will usually blossom in early spring.

1 Prepare the barbecue. Boil the potatoes in a large pan of lightly salted water for about 10 minutes, or until just tender. Meanwhile, make the dressing by whisking the vinegar with 75ml/ 5 tbsp of the oil, then stirring in the chives and flowers. Drain the potatoes and cut them in half. Season to taste.

2 Position a lightly oiled grill rack over the hot coals. Toss the potatoes in the remaining oil and lay them on the grill rack over medium-high heat, cut-side down. Leave for about 5 minutes, then press down a little so that they are imprinted with the marks of the grill.

3 Turn the potatoes over and cook the second side for about 3 minutes. Place the potatoes in a bowl, pour over the dressing and toss lightly to mix.

4 Grill the tomatoes for 3 minutes, or until they are just beginning to blister. Serve with the potatoes, which can be hot, warm or cold.

Energy 232kcal/970kJ; Protein 3g; Carbohydrate 26.2g, of which sugars 4g; Fat 13.5g, of which saturates 2.1g; Cholesterol 0mg; Calcium 14mg; Fibre 2.2g; Sodium 23mg.

HUSK-GRILLED CORN <u>ON THE</u> COB

KEEPING THE HUSKS ON THE CORN PROTECTS THE KERNELS AND ENCLOSES THE BUTTER, SO THE FLAVOURS ARE CONTAINED. FRESH CORN WITH HUSKS INTACT ARE PERFECT, BUT BANANA LEAVES OR A DOUBLE LAYER OF FOIL ARE ALSO SUITABLE.

SERVES SIX

INGREDIENTS
  3 dried chipotle chillies
  250g/9oz/generous 1 cup butter,
  softened
  7.5ml/1½ tsp lemon juice
  45ml/3 tbsp chopped fresh flat
  leaf parsley
  6 corn on the cob, with husks intact
  salt and ground black pepper

1 Heat a heavy frying pan. Add the dried chillies and roast them by stirring them continuously for 1 minute without letting them scorch. Put them in a bowl with almost boiling water to cover. Use a saucer to keep them submerged, and leave them to rehydrate for up to 1 hour. Drain, remove the seeds and chop the chillies finely. Place the butter in a bowl and add the chillies, lemon juice and parsley. Season and mix well.

2 Peel back the husks from each cob without tearing them. Remove the silk. Smear about 30ml/2 tbsp of the chilli butter over each cob. Pull the husks back over the cobs, ensuring that the butter is well hidden. Put the rest of the butter in a pot, smooth the top and chill to use later. Place the cobs in a bowl of cold water and leave in a cool place for 1–3 hours; longer if that suits your work plan better.

3 Prepare the barbecue. Remove the corn cobs from the water and wrap in pairs in foil. Position a lightly oiled grill rack over the hot coals. Grill the corn over medium-high heat for 15–20 minutes until softened.

4 Remove the foil and cook them for about 5 minutes more, turning them often to char the husks a little. Serve hot, with the rest of the chilli butter.

Energy 435kcal/1805kJ; Protein 3.4g; Carbohydrate 27.1g, of which sugars 10.1g; Fat 35.6g, of which saturates 21.9g; Cholesterol 89mg; Calcium 28mg; Fibre 1.8g; Sodium 525mg.

ROASTED BEETROOT WITH GARLIC SAUCE

BEETROOT HAS A LOVELY SWEET AND EARTHY FLAVOUR THAT IS MOST PRONOUNCED WHEN IT IS ROASTED. IN GREECE IT IS OFTEN SERVED WITH A GARLIC SAUCE CALLED SKORTHALIA, WHICH CONTRASTS BEAUTIFULLY WITH THE SWEETNESS OF THE BEETROOT.

2 While the blender or processor is running, drizzle in the olive oil through the lid or feeder tube. The sauce should be runny. Spoon it into a serving bowl and set it aside.

3 Prepare the barbecue. Rinse the beetroot under running water to remove any grit, but be careful not to pierce the skin or the colour will run.

4 Wrap the beetroot in groups of 3 or 4 in a double thickness of heavy-duty foil and leave the tops open. Drizzle over a little of the oil and sprinkle lightly with salt.

5 Close up the parcels and arrange them among the coals heated to medium-high. Bake for about 1½ hours until perfectly soft.

6 Remove the beetroot from the foil parcels. When they are just cool enough to handle, peel them. Slice them in thin round slices and serve with the remaining oil drizzled all over.

7 To serve, either spread a thin layer of garlic sauce on top, or hand it around separately. Serve with fresh bread, if you like.

SERVES FOUR

INGREDIENTS
675g/1½lb medium or small
    beetroot (beets)
75–90ml/5–6 tbsp extra virgin
    olive oil
salt
For the garlic sauce
    4 medium slices of bread, crusts
        removed, soaked in water for
        10 minutes
    2–3 garlic cloves, chopped
    15ml/1 tbsp white wine vinegar
    60ml/4 tbsp extra virgin olive oil

1 To make the garlic sauce, squeeze most of the water out of the bread, but leave it quite moist. Place it in a blender or food processor. Add the garlic and vinegar, with salt to taste, and blend until smooth.

Energy 344kcal/1435kJ; Protein 5.1g; Carbohydrate 25.7g, of which sugars 12.5g; Fat 25.4g, of which saturates 3.6g; Cholesterol 0mg; Calcium 62mg; Fibre 3.6g; Sodium 247mg.

ROASTED ONIONS WITH SUN-DRIED TOMATOES

ONIONS ROAST TO A WONDERFUL SWEET CREAMINESS WHEN COOKED IN THEIR SKINS. THEY NEED BUTTER, LOTS OF BLACK PEPPER AND SALTY FOOD TO SET OFF THEIR SWEETNESS. LET THEM COOK AWAY NEXT TO THE COALS WHILE YOU USE THE GRILL RACK TO COOK YOUR ACCOMPANYING DISH.

SERVES SIX

INGREDIENTS
  6 even-sized red onions, unpeeled
  olive oil, for drizzling
  175–225g/6–8oz crumbly cheese
    (such as Lancashire, Caerphilly or
    Cheshire), thinly sliced
  a few snipped chives
  salt and ground black pepper
For the sun-dried tomato butter
  115g/4oz/½ cup butter, softened
  65g/2½oz sun-dried tomatoes in
    olive oil, drained and finely chopped
  30ml/2 tbsp chopped fresh basil
    or parsley

VARIATIONS
• Use goat's cheese instead of
Lancashire, Caerphilly or Cheshire.
• Fry fresh white breadcrumbs in butter
with a little garlic until crisp and then
mix with lots of chopped fresh parsley.
Scatter the crisp crumb mixture over the
onions before serving.

1 To make the sun-dried tomato butter,
cream the butter and then beat in the
tomatoes and basil or parsley. Season to
taste with salt and pepper and shape
into a roll, then wrap in foil and chill.

2 Prepare the barbecue. Wrap the
unpeeled onions separately in a double
thickness of heavy-duty foil, leaving the
top open. Drizzle in a little oil then
close. Place the parcels among the
coals heated to medium-high and cook
for 1 hour, or until they are tender and
feel soft when lightly squeezed.

3 Slit the tops of the onions and open
them up. Season with plenty of black
pepper and add chunks of the sun-
dried tomato butter. Scatter the cheese
and chives over the top and eat
immediately, mashing the butter and
cheese into the soft, sweet onion.

COOK'S TIP
If you only have dry sun-dried tomatoes,
you will need to soften them in boiling
water beforehand.

Energy 304kcal/1258kJ; Protein 9g; Carbohydrate 8.6g, of which sugars 6.3g; Fat 25.6g, of which saturates 16.3g; Cholesterol 69mg; Calcium 260mg; Fibre 1.9g; Sodium 334mg.

TRADITIONAL COLESLAW

EVERY DELI SELLS COLESLAW BUT THERE IS BORING COLESLAW AND EXCITING COLESLAW. THE KEY TO GOOD COLESLAW IS A ZESTY DRESSING AND AN INTERESTING SELECTION OF VEGETABLES. THINLY SLICED CABBAGE IS ALSO ESSENTIAL AND IS BEST DONE USING A MANDOLIN, IF YOU HAVE ONE.

SERVES SIX TO EIGHT

INGREDIENTS
1 large white or green cabbage, very
   thinly sliced
3–4 carrots, coarsely grated
½ red and ½ green (bell) pepper,
   chopped
1–2 celery sticks, finely chopped or
   5–10ml/1–2 tsp celery seeds
1 onion, chopped
2–3 handfuls of raisins or sultanas
   (golden raisins)
45ml/3 tbsp white wine vinegar or
   cider vinegar
60–90ml/4–6 tbsp sugar, to taste
175–250ml/6–8fl oz/¾–1 cup
   mayonnaise, to bind
salt and ground black pepper

1 Put the cabbage, carrots, peppers, celery or celery seeds, onion, and raisins or sultanas in a salad bowl and mix to combine well. Add the vinegar, sugar, salt and ground black pepper and toss together well until thoroughly combined. Leave to stand for about 1 hour.

2 Stir enough mayonnaise into the salad to bind the ingredients together lightly. Taste the salad for seasoning and sweet-and-sour flavour, adding more sugar, salt and pepper if needed. Chill. Drain off any excess liquid from the salad before serving.

Energy 222kcal/921kJ; Protein 2g; Carbohydrate 16.1g, of which sugars 15.4g; Fat 17g, of which saturates 2.6g; Cholesterol 16mg; Calcium 55mg; Fibre 3.4g; Sodium 120mg.

THE ULTIMATE DELI-STYLE SALAD

A LOVELY CHUNKY SALAD, TOSSED IN A LIGHT, CREAMY DRESSING AND FRESH WITH PIQUANT FLAVOURS, IS A MUST-HAVE FOR ANY BARBECUE SPREAD. IT IS TEMPTING TO POP ALONG TO YOUR LOCAL DELI FOR SOMETHING READY-PREPARED, BUT YOU CAN MAKE THIS VERY ONE EASILY AT HOME.

SERVES SIX TO EIGHT

INGREDIENTS
1kg/2¼lb waxy salad
   potatoes, scrubbed
1 red or white onion, finely chopped
2–3 celery sticks, finely chopped
60–90ml/4–6 tbsp chopped
   fresh parsley
15–20 pimiento-stuffed olives, halved
3 hard-boiled eggs, chopped
60ml/4 tbsp extra virgin olive oil
60ml/4 tbsp white wine vinegar
15–30ml/1–2 tbsp mild or
   wholegrain mustard
celery seeds, to taste (optional)
175–250ml/6–8fl oz/
   ¾–1 cup mayonnaise
salt and ground black pepper
paprika, to garnish

1 Cook the potatoes in a pan of salted boiling water until tender. Drain, return to the pan and leave for 2–3 minutes to cool and dry a little.

2 When the potatoes are cool enough to handle but still very warm, cut them into chunks or slices and place in a salad bowl.

3 Sprinkle the potatoes with salt and pepper, then add the onion, celery, parsley, olives and the chopped eggs. In a jug (pitcher), combine the olive oil, vinegar, mustard and celery seeds, if using, pour over the salad and toss to combine. Add enough mayonnaise to bind the salad together. Chill before serving, sprinkled with a little paprika.

Energy 331kcal/1375kJ; Protein 5.1g; Carbohydrate 21.4g, of which sugars 2.6g; Fat 25.6g, of which saturates 4.2g; Cholesterol 88mg; Calcium 45mg; Fibre 2.1g; Sodium 358mg.

SALAD WITH WATERMELON AND FETA CHEESE

THE COMBINATION OF SWEET AND JUICY WATERMELON WITH SALTY FETA CHEESE IS AN ISRAELI ORIGINAL AND WAS INSPIRED BY THE TURKISH TRADITION OF EATING WATERMELON WITH SALTY WHITE CHEESE IN THE HOT SUMMER MONTHS. IT'S JUST GREAT WITH BARBECUED FOOD.

SERVES FOUR

INGREDIENTS

30–45ml/2–3 tbsp extra virgin
  olive oil
juice of ½ lemon
5ml/1 tsp vinegar to taste
sprinkling of fresh thyme
pinch of ground cumin
4 large slices of watermelon, chilled
1 frisée lettuce, core removed
130g/4½oz feta cheese,
  preferably sheep's milk feta,
  cut into bite size pieces
handful of lightly toasted
  pumpkin seeds
handful of sunflower seeds
10–15 black olives

1 Pour the extra virgin olive oil, lemon juice and vinegar into a bowl or jug (pitcher). Add the fresh thyme and ground cumin, and whisk until well combined. Cover the dressing and set aside until you are ready to serve the salad, but do not chill.

2 Cut the rind off the watermelon and remove as many seeds as possible. Cut the flesh into triangular-shaped chunks.

3 Put the lettuce leaves in a bowl, pour over the dressing and toss together. Arrange the leaves on a serving dish or individual plates and add the watermelon, feta cheese, pumpkin and sunflower seeds, and the black olives. Serve the salad immediately.

COOK'S TIP
The best choice of olives for this recipe are plump black Mediterranean olives such as Kalamata, and other shiny, brined varieties or dry-cured black olives such as Italian varieties.

Energy 242kcal/1006kJ; Protein 7.9g; Carbohydrate 11.4g, of which sugars 9.7g; Fat 18.6g, of which saturates 6g; Cholesterol 23mg; Calcium 147mg; Fibre 1.2g; Sodium 752mg.

WILD GREEN SALAD

A MIXTURE OF SALAD LEAVES MAKES A REFRESHING ACCOMPANIMENT TO A MEAL, ESPECIALLY WHEN YOU CHOOSE THOSE THAT HAVE CONTRASTING FLAVOURS, LIKE THE ONES USED HERE. THE SALAD IS LIGHTLY DRESSED AND GOES WELL WITH A YOGURT AND FETA CHEESE ACCOMPANIMENT.

SERVES FOUR

INGREDIENTS
1 large bunch wild rocket (arugula), about 115g/4oz
1 packet mixed salad leaves
¼ white cabbage, thinly sliced
1 cucumber, sliced
1 small red onion, chopped
2–3 garlic cloves, chopped
3–5 tomatoes, cut into wedges
1 green (bell) pepper, seeded and sliced
2–3 mint sprigs, sliced or torn
15–30ml/1–2 tbsp chopped fresh parsley and/or tarragon or dill
pinch of dried oregano or thyme
45ml/3 tbsp extra virgin olive oil
juice of ½ lemon
15ml/1 tbsp red wine vinegar
15–20 black olives
salt and ground black pepper

1 In a large salad bowl, put the rocket, mixed salad leaves, white cabbage, cucumber, onion and garlic. Toss gently with your fingers to combine the leaves and vegetables.

COOK'S TIP
If you like, accompany this salad with 50g/2oz of crumbled feta cheese mixed into 115g/4oz natural (plain) yogurt and sprinkled with paprika.

2 Arrange the tomatoes, pepper, mint, fresh and dried herbs, salt and pepper on top of the greens and vegetables. Drizzle over the oil, lemon juice and vinegar, stud with the olives and serve.

VARIATION
For a tomato salad, omit the cabbage, use fewer salad leaves and substitute 450g/1lb ripe cherry tomatoes for the tomatoes in the recipe.

Energy 146kcal/605kJ; Protein 3.1g; Carbohydrate 10g, of which sugars 9.4g; Fat 10.6g, of which saturates 1.6g; Cholesterol 0mg; Calcium 99mg; Fibre 3.9g; Sodium 337mg.

HUMMUS

THIS CLASSIC MIDDLE EASTERN DISH IS MADE FROM COOKED CHICKPEAS GROUND TO A PASTE AND FLAVOURED WITH GARLIC, LEMON JUICE, TAHINI, OLIVE OIL AND CUMIN. IT IS DELICIOUS SERVED WITH WEDGES OF TOASTED PITTA BREAD OR CRUDITÉS.

SERVES FOUR TO SIX

INGREDIENTS
    400g/14oz can chickpeas, drained
    60ml/4 tbsp tahini
    2–3 garlic cloves, chopped
    juice of ½–1 lemon
    cayenne pepper
    small pinch to 1.5ml/¼ tsp ground
       cumin, or more to taste
    salt and ground black pepper

VARIATION
Process 2 roasted red (bell) peppers with the chickpeas, then continue as above. Serve sprinkled with lightly toasted pine nuts and paprika mixed with olive oil.

1 Using a potato masher or food processor, coarsely mash the chickpeas. If you prefer a smoother purée, process them in a food processor or blender until smooth.

2 Mix the tahini into the chickpeas, then stir in the remaining ingredients, and salt and pepper to taste. If needed, add a little water. Serve at room temperature with grilled pittas.

Energy 144kcal/603kJ; Protein 7.2g; Carbohydrate 11.9g, of which sugars 0.4g; Fat 7.9g, of which saturates 1.1g; Cholesterol 0mg; Calcium 98mg; Fibre 3.8g; Sodium 149mg

GUACAMOLE

ONE OF THE BEST-LOVED MEXICAN SALSAS, THIS BLEND OF CREAMY AVOCADO, TOMATOES, CHILLIES, CORIANDER AND LIME NOW APPEARS ON TABLES THE WORLD OVER. SERVE WITH VEGETABLE CRUDITÉS, TORTILLA CHIPS OR BREADSTICKS, OR SERVE AS A CLASSIC ACCOMPANIMENT TO FAJITAS.

SERVES SIX TO EIGHT

INGREDIENTS
 4 tomatoes
 4 ripe avocados, preferably *fuerte*
 freshly squeezed juice of 1 lime
 ½ small onion, finely chopped
 2 garlic cloves, crushed
 small bunch of fresh coriander
  (cilantro), chopped
 3 fresh red fresno chillies
 salt
 tortilla chips or breadsticks, to serve

COOK'S TIP
Smooth-skinned *fuerte* avocados are native to Mexico, so would be ideal for this dip. If they are not available, use any avocados, but make sure that they are ripe. To test, gently press the top of the avocado; it should give a little.

1 Cut a cross in the base of each tomato. Place the tomatoes in a heatproof bowl and pour over boiling water to cover.

2 Leave the tomatoes in the water for 30 seconds, then lift them out using a slotted spoon and plunge them into a bowl of cold water. Drain. The skins will have begun to peel back from the crosses. Remove the skins completely. Cut the tomatoes in half, remove the seeds with a teaspoon, then chop the flesh roughly and set it aside.

3 Cut the avocados in half then remove the stones (pits). Scoop the flesh out of the shells and place it in a food processor or blender. Process the pulp until almost smooth, then scrape into a bowl and stir in the lime juice.

4 Add the onion and garlic to the avocado and mix well. Stir in the coriander until combined.

5 Remove the stalks from the chillies, slit them and scrape out the seeds with a small, sharp knife. Chop the chillies finely and add them to the avocado mixture, with the roughly chopped tomatoes. Mix well.

6 Taste the guacamole and add salt, if needed. Cover closely with clear film (plastic wrap) or a tight-fitting lid and chill for 1 hour before serving as a dip with tortilla chips or breadsticks. If it is well covered, guacamole will keep in the refrigerator for 2–3 days.

Energy 108kcal/449kJ; Protein 1.6g; Carbohydrate 3.3g, of which sugars 2.4g; Fat 9.9g, of which saturates 2.1g; Cholesterol 0mg; Calcium 23mg; Fibre 2.6g; Sodium 10mg.

CHILLI RELISH

BURGERS OR BARBECUED SAUSAGES TASTE GREAT WITH A SPICY RELISH, AND A HOME-MADE ONE IS SO MUCH NICER THAN ONE FROM A JAR. THIS CHILLI RELISH WILL LAST FOR AT LEAST A WEEK STORED IN A REFRIGERATOR, SO YOU COULD MAKE IT A FEW DAYS IN ADVANCE OF YOUR BARBECUE.

2 Heat the olive oil in a pan. Add the onion, red pepper and garlic to the pan.

3 Cook the vegetables gently for 5–8 minutes, or until the pepper is softened. Add the chopped tomatoes, cover and cook for 5 minutes, until the tomatoes release their juices.

4 Stir in the remaining ingredients except for the basil. Bring gently to the boil, stirring, until the sugar dissolves.

5 Simmer, uncovered, for 20 minutes, or until the mixture is pulpy. Stir in the basil leaves and check the seasoning.

6 Allow to cool completely, then transfer to a glass jar or a plastic container with a tightly fitting lid. Store, covered, in the refrigerator.

SERVES EIGHT

INGREDIENTS
    6 tomatoes
    30ml/2 tbsp olive oil
    1 onion, roughly chopped
    1 red (bell) pepper, seeded
       and chopped
    2 garlic cloves, chopped
    5ml/1 tsp ground cinnamon
    5ml/1 tsp chilli flakes
    5ml/1 tsp ground ginger
    5ml/1 tsp salt
    2.5ml/½ tsp ground black pepper
    75g/3oz/⅓ cup light muscovado
       (brown) sugar
    75ml/5 tbsp cider vinegar
    handful of fresh basil leaves, chopped

1 Skewer each tomato on a metal fork and hold in a gas flame for 1–2 minutes, turning, until the skin splits and wrinkles. Alternatively, plunge the tomatoes into boiling water for 30 seconds, then refresh in cold water. Peel away the skins and roughly chop the flesh.

COOK'S TIP
This relish thickens slightly on cooling so do not worry if the mixture seems a little wet at the end of step 6.

Energy 84kcal/355kJ; Protein 0.9g; Carbohydrate 14.1g, of which sugars 13.9g; Fat 3.1g, of which saturates 0.5g; Cholesterol 0mg; Calcium 14mg; Fibre 1.2g; Sodium 8mg.

TZATZIKI

THIS CLASSIC GREEK DIP IS A COOLING MIX OF YOGURT, CUCUMBER AND MINT, PERFECT FOR A HOT SUMMER'S DAY. SERVE IT WITH STRIPS OF LIGHTLY TOASTED PITTA BREAD OR USE IT TO ACCOMPANY BARBECUED VEGETABLES. IT ALSO MAKES A TASTY ADDITION TO A SALAD SELECTION.

SERVES FOUR

INGREDIENTS
    1 mini cucumber
    4 spring onions (scallions)
    1 garlic clove
    200ml/7fl oz/scant 1 cup Greek
      (US strained plain) yogurt
    45ml/3 tbsp chopped fresh mint
    salt and ground black pepper
    fresh mint sprig, to garnish (optional)

3 Beat the yogurt until smooth, if necessary, then gently stir in the cucumber, onions, garlic and mint.

4 Season to taste, then transfer the mixture to a serving bowl. Chill until ready to serve with pitta breads.

1 Trim the ends from the cucumber, then cut it into 5mm/¼in dice. Set aside.

2 Trim the spring onions and garlic, then chop both very finely.

COOK'S TIP
• Use Greek (US strained plain) yogurt for this dip – it has a higher fat content than most yogurts, but this gives it a deliciously rich, creamy texture.
• Mint or coriander (cilantro) leaves will make a suitable garnish for this recipe.

Energy 62kcal/258kJ; Protein 3.6g; Carbohydrate 1.7g, of which sugars 1.6g; Fat 5.2g, of which saturates 2.6g; Cholesterol 0mg; Calcium 84mg; Fibre 0.3g; Sodium 37mg.

QUICK SATAY SAUCE

THERE ARE MANY VERSIONS OF THIS TASTY PEANUT SAUCE. THIS ONE IS VERY SPEEDY AND IT TASTES DELICIOUS DRIZZLED OVER BARBECUED SKEWERS OF CHICKEN. FOR PARTIES, SPEAR CHUNKS OF CHICKEN WITH COCKTAIL STICKS AND ARRANGE AROUND A BOWL OF WARM SAUCE.

2 Add the peanut butter and stir vigorously until it is blended into the coconut cream. Continue to heat until the mixture is warm but not boiling hot.

3 Add the Worcestershire sauce and a dash of Tabasco to taste. Pour into a serving bowl.

4 Use a potato peeler to shave thin curls from a piece of fresh coconut, if using. Scatter the coconut over the dish of your choice and serve immediately with the sauce.

SERVES FOUR

INGREDIENTS
200ml/7fl oz/scant 1 cup coconut cream
60ml/4 tbsp crunchy peanut butter
5ml/1 tsp Worcestershire sauce
Tabasco sauce, to taste
fresh coconut, to garnish (optional)

COOK'S TIP
Thick coconut milk can be substituted for coconut cream, but take care to buy an unsweetened variety for this recipe.

1 Pour the coconut cream into a small pan and heat it gently over a low heat for about 2 minutes.

Energy 108kcal/451kJ; Protein 3.6g; Carbohydrate 5.8g, of which sugars 4.9g; Fat 8g, of which saturates 2.1g; Cholesterol 0mg; Calcium 30mg; Fibre 0.8g; Sodium 150mg.

SPICED TAMARIND MUSTARD

TAMARIND HAS A DISTINCTIVE SWEET AND SOUR FLAVOUR, A DARK BROWN COLOUR AND STICKY TEXTURE. COMBINED WITH SPICES AND GROUND MUSTARD SEEDS, IT MAKES A WONDERFUL CONDIMENT. SERVE WITH STEAKS AND GRILLED MEATS.

MAKES ABOUT 200G/7OZ

INGREDIENTS
  115g/4oz tamarind block
  150ml/¼ pint/⅔ cup warm water
  50g/2oz/¼ cup yellow mustard seeds
  25ml/1½ tbsp black or brown
    mustard seeds
  10ml/2 tsp clear honey
  pinch of ground cardamom
  pinch of salt

COOK'S TIP
The mustard will be ready to eat in 3–4 days. It should be stored in a cool, dark place and used within 4 months.

1 Put the tamarind in a small bowl and pour over the water. Leave to soak for 30 minutes. Mash to a pulp with a fork, then strain through a fine sieve into a bowl.

2 Grind the mustard seeds in a spice mill or coffee grinder and add to the tamarind with the remaining ingredients. Spoon into sterilized jars, cover and seal.

Energy 262kcal/1095kJ; Protein 15g; Carbohydrate 18.9g, of which sugars 8.5g; Fat 22.8g, of which saturates 0.8g; Cholesterol 2mg; Calcium 207mg; Fibre 1.1g; Sodium 64mg.

CORN TORTILLAS

THESE DELICIOUS AND VERSATILE MEXICAN SPECIALITIES COOK VERY QUICKLY. GRIDDLE THEM OVER THE BARBECUE AND HAVE A CLEAN DISH TOWEL ON HAND TO KEEP THE HOT STACKS WARM.

MAKES ABOUT FOURTEEN

INGREDIENTS
275g/10oz/2½ cups masa harina
250–350ml/8–12fl oz/
  1–1½ cups water

COOK'S TIPS
• When making tortillas, it is important to get the dough texture right. If it is too dry and crumbly, add a little water; if it is too wet, add more masa harina. If you do not manage to flatten the ball of dough into a neat circle the first time, just re-roll it and try again.
• These tortillas can also be cooked in the oven at 150°C/300°F/Gas 2.

1 Prepare the barbecue. Put the masa harina into a bowl and stir in 250ml/ 8fl oz/1 cup of the measured water, mixing it to a soft dough that just holds together. If it is too dry, add a little more water. Cover the bowl with a cloth and set aside for 15 minutes.

2 Knead the dough lightly, divide into 14 pieces, and shape into balls.

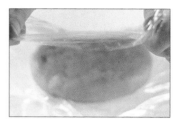

3 Using a rolling pin, roll out each ball between sheets of clear plastic film until you have a thin round of dough measuring about 15cm/6in in diameter.

4 Put a griddle over the hot coals and griddle the first tortilla for 1 minute. Turn it over and cook for a minute more. Wrap in a clean dish towel and keep warm. Repeat for the other tortillas.

COOK'S TIP
An alternative to rolling out rounds of tortilla dough with a rolling pin is to use a tortilla press. Open the press and line both sides with sheets of clear plastic film. Shape the tortilla dough into balls, put one ball on the press and bring the top down firmly to flatten it into a neat round. Open the press, peel off the top layer of plastic and, using the bottom layer, lift the tortilla out of the press. Peel off this layer of plastic and repeat the process with the other dough balls.

Energy 72kcal/303kJ; Protein 1.9g; Carbohydrate 14.4g, of which sugars 0g; Fat 0.7g, of which saturates 0g; Cholesterol 0mg; Calcium 1mg; Fibre 0.4g; Sodium 0mg.

FLOUR TORTILLAS

HOME-MADE TORTILLAS TASTE SO GOOD FILLED WITH BARBECUED VEGETABLES AND THINLY SLICED CHICKEN OR MEAT. YOU CAN MAKE THEM IN ADVANCE AND THEN REHEAT THEM TO SERVE.

MAKES ABOUT FOURTEEN

INGREDIENTS
225g/8oz/2 cups plain
   (all-purpose) flour
5ml/1 tsp salt
15ml/1 tbsp lard or white cooking fat
120ml/4fl oz/½ cup water

1 Sift the flour and salt into a large mixing bowl. Gradually rub in the lard or white cooking fat using your fingertips until the mixture resembles coarse breadcrumbs.

2 Gradually add the water and mix to a soft dough. Knead lightly, form into a ball, cover with a cloth and leave to rest for 15 minutes. Prepare the barbecue.

COOK'S TIPS
• Make flour tortillas whenever masa harina is difficult to find. To keep them soft and pliable, make sure they are kept warm until ready to serve, and eat as soon as possible.
• These flour tortillas can also be cooked in the oven at 150°C/300°F/Gas 2.

3 Carefully divide the dough into about 14 portions and form these portions into small balls. One by one, roll out each ball of dough on a lightly floured wooden board to a round measuring about 15cm/6in. Trim the rounds if necessary.

4 Heat an ungreased flat griddle or frying pan over a medium heat. Cook the tortillas for about 1½–2 minutes on each side. Turn over with a palette knife or metal spatula when the bottom begins to brown. Wrap in a clean dish towel to keep warm until ready to serve.

Energy 64kcal/272kJ; Protein 1.5g; Carbohydrate 12.5g, of which sugars 0.2g; Fat 1.3g, of which saturates 0.5g; Cholesterol 1mg; Calcium 23mg; Fibre 0.5g; Sodium 141mg.

PITTA BREAD

FOR A RELAXED BARBECUE WHERE FINGERS ARE KEPT FAIRLY CLEAN, YOU CAN'T BEAT SERVING TASTY SLICES OR CHUNKS OF FOOD IN PITTA BREAD POCKETS. YOU CAN MAKE THE DOUGH EARLIER AND THEN COOK IT IN A HEAVY FRYING PAN ON THE BARBECUE.

5 Prepare the barbecue. Heat a large, heavy frying pan over a medium-high heat. When it is smoking hot, gently lay one piece of flattened dough in the pan and cook for 15–20 seconds. Carefully turn it over and cook the second side for about 1 minute.

6 When large bubbles start to form on the bread, turn it over again. It should puff up. Using a clean dish towel, gently press on the bread where the bubbles have formed. Cook for a total of 3 minutes, then remove the pitta from the pan. Repeat with the remaining dough until all the breads have been cooked.

7 Wrap the pitta breads in a clean dish towel, stacking them as each one is cooked. Serve the pitta breads hot while they are soft and moist.

MAKES TWELVE

INGREDIENTS

500g/1¼lb/4½ cups strong white bread flour, or half white and half wholemeal (whole-wheat)
7g/¼oz packet easy-blend (rapid-rise) dried yeast
15ml/1 tbsp salt
15ml/1 tbsp olive oil
250ml/8fl oz/1 cup water

1 Combine the flour, yeast and salt. In a large bowl, mix together the oil and water, then stir in half of the flour mixture, stirring in the same direction, until the dough is stiff. Knead in the remaining flour.

2 Place the dough in a clean bowl, cover with a clean dish towel and leave in a warm place for at least 30 minutes and up to 2 hours.

3 Knead the dough for 10 minutes, or until smooth. Lightly oil the bowl, place the dough in it, cover again and leave to rise in a warm place for about 1 hour, or until doubled in size.

4 Divide the dough into 12 equal-size pieces. With lightly floured hands, flatten each piece, then roll out into a round about 20cm/8in in diameter and about 5mm–1cm/¼–½in thick. Keep the rolled breads covered with a clean dish towel while you make the remaining breads.

VARIATION

To cook the breads in the oven, preheat the oven to 220°C/425°F/Gas 7. Fill an unglazed or partially glazed dish with hot water and place in the bottom of the oven. Alternatively, arrange a handful of unglazed tiles in the bottom of the oven. Use either a non-stick baking sheet or a lightly oiled ordinary baking sheet and heat in the oven for a few minutes. Place two or three pieces of flattened dough on to the hot baking sheet and place in the hottest part of the oven. Bake for 2–3 minutes. They should puff up. Repeat with the remaining dough until all the pittas have been cooked.

Energy 150kcal/638kJ; Protein 3.9g; Carbohydrate 32.4g, of which sugars 0.6g; Fat 1.5g, of which saturates 0.2g; Cholesterol 0mg; Calcium 59mg; Fibre 1.3g; Sodium 493mg.

CIABATTA

THE VERY WET DOUGH USED TO MAKE CIABATTA BREAD RESULTS IN A LIGHT AND AIRY CRUMB. CIABATTA IS ONE OF THE MOST POPULAR BREADS AND TASTES WONDERFUL WHEN HOME-MADE. IT CAN BE USED AS AN ACCOMPANIMENT TO BARBECUED FOOD OR SLICED, TOPPED WITH DELICIOUS MORSELS AND GRILLED.

MAKES THREE LOAVES

INGREDIENTS
For the starter
   7g/¼oz fresh yeast
   175–200ml/6–7fl oz/¾–scant 1 cup
     lukewarm water
   350g/12oz/3 cups unbleached strong
     white bread flour, plus extra
     for dusting
For the dough
   15g/½oz fresh yeast
   400ml/14fl oz/1⅔ cups
     lukewarm water
   60ml/4 tbsp lukewarm milk
   500g/1¼lb/5 cups unbleached strong
     white bread flour
   10ml/2 tsp salt
   45ml/3 tbsp extra virgin olive oil

1 For the starter, cream the yeast with a little of the measured water. Sift the flour into a large bowl. Gradually mix in the yeast mixture and sufficient of the remaining water to form a firm dough.

2 Turn out the starter dough on to a lightly floured surface and knead for about 5 minutes until smooth and elastic. Return the dough to the bowl, cover with lightly oiled clear film (plastic wrap) and leave in a warm place for 12–15 hours, or until the dough has risen and is starting to collapse.

3 Sprinkle three baking sheets with flour. Mix the yeast for the dough with a little of the measured water until creamy, then mix in the remainder. Add the yeast mixture to the starter and gradually mix in.

4 Mix in the milk, beating thoroughly with a wooden spoon. Using your hand, gradually incorporate the flour, lifting the dough as you mix. Mixing the dough will take 15 minutes or more and it forms a very wet mix, which is impossible to knead on a work surface.

5 Beat in the salt and olive oil. Cover with lightly oiled clear film and leave to rise, in a warm place, for 1½–2 hours, or until doubled in bulk.

6 With a spoon, carefully tip one-third of the dough at a time on to the baking sheets without knocking back (punching down) the dough in the process.

7 Using floured hands, shape into rough oblong loaf shapes, about 2.5cm/1in thick. Flatten slightly with splayed fingers. Sprinkle with flour and leave to rise in a warm place for 30 minutes.

8 Meanwhile, preheat the oven to 220°C/425°F/Gas 7. Bake for 25–30 minutes, or until golden brown and sounding hollow when tapped on the base. Transfer to a wire rack to cool.

Energy 1074kcal/4554kJ; Protein 27.3g; Carbohydrate 221.1g, of which sugars 5.2g; Fat 15g, of which saturates 2.4g; Cholesterol 1mg; Calcium 421mg; Fibre 8.8g; Sodium 1327mg.

DESSERTS AND DRINKS

The main course is ready, the coals are still hot, so why not use the barbecue to grill or bake some mouthwatering desserts? Firm-fleshed fruits such as melons, pineapples and mangoes can easily be cooked on the grill rack or griddle and then served with a sauce or ice cream, but soft fruits can also be cooked on the barbecue. Try the recipe for strawberries cooked on cherry wood skewers with toasted marshmallows — a heavenly combination that adults as well as children will love. You can also wrap fruits in foil and bake them on the grill; to make them extra special, serve them with a sauce or ice cream. If you want to prepare the dessert completely in advance, a simple salad of exotic fruits will make an excellent end to a satisfying barbecued meal. Also included in this chapter are some refreshing non-alcoholic drinks that are just right for a warm summer's day socializing with friends or enjoying a relaxing time outdoors with the family around the barbecue.

GRILLED STRAWBERRIES AND MARSHMALLOWS

IT IS ALWAYS A TREAT TO HAVE PERMISSION TO EAT MARSHMALLOWS. AFTER COOKING, DREDGE THESE LITTLE KEBABS WITH LOADS OF ICING SUGAR, SOME OF WHICH WILL MELT INTO THE STRAWBERRY JUICE. THE GRILL HAS TO BE VERY HOT TO SEAR THE MARSHMALLOWS QUICKLY BEFORE THEY MELT.

SERVES FOUR

INGREDIENTS

16 mixed pink and white
   marshmallows, chilled
16 strawberries
icing (confectioners') sugar
   for dusting
8 short lengths of cherry wood or
   metal skewers

COOK'S TIP

By chilling the marshmallows for at least half an hour, they will be firmer and easier to thread on to the skewers.

1 Prepare the barbecue. If you are using cherry wood skewers, soak them in water for 30 minutes. Position a lightly oiled grill rack just above the hot coals to heat.

2 Spike 2 marshmallows and 2 strawberries on each drained cherry wood or metal skewer and grill over the hot coals for 20 seconds on each side. If nice grill marks don't appear easily, don't persist for too long or the marsh-mallows may burn – cook until they are warm to the touch and only just beginning to melt.

3 Transfer the skewered strawberries and marshmallows to individual dessert plates or a large platter, dust generously with icing sugar and serve.

Energy 110kcal/466kJ; Protein 1.4g; Carbohydrate 27.6g, of which sugars 22.9g; Fat 0.1g, of which saturates 0g; Cholesterol 0mg; Calcium 11mg; Fibre 0.5g; Sodium 10mg

HONEY-SEARED MELON

THIS FABULOUSLY SIMPLE DESSERT CAN BE MADE WITH MELON THAT IS SLIGHTLY UNDERRIPE, BECAUSE THE HONEYCOMB WILL SWEETEN IT UP BEAUTIFULLY. IT'S IDEAL TO MAKE DURING THE SUMMER WHEN RASPBERRIES ARE IN SEASON AND LAVENDER IN FLOWER.

SERVES SIX

INGREDIENTS
    1.3kg/3lb melon, preferably
      Charentais
    200g/7oz honeycomb
    5ml/1 tsp water
    a bunch of lavender, plus extra
      flowers for decoration
    300g/11oz/2 cups raspberries

COOK'S TIP
Make sure that the lavender you use in
this recipe is fresh.

1 Prepare the barbecue. Cut the melon in half, scoop out the seeds then cut each half into three slices. Put a third of the honeycomb in a bowl and dilute by stirring in the water. Make a brush with the lavender and dip it into the honey.

2 Heat a griddle on the grill rack over hot coals. Lightly brush the melon with the honey mixture. Grill for 30 seconds on each side. Serve hot, sprinkled with the raspberries and remaining lavender flowers, and topped with the remaining honeycomb.

Energy 113kcal/480kJ; Protein 1.9g; Carbohydrate 27.2g, of which sugars 27.2g; Fat 0.4g, of which saturates 0.1g; Cholesterol 0mg; Calcium 42mg; Fibre 2.1g; Sodium 71mg.

GRILLED MANGO SLICES WITH LIME SORBET

IF YOU CAN LOCATE THEM, USE ALPHONSO MANGOES FOR THIS DISH. MAINLY CULTIVATED IN INDIA, THEY HAVE A HEADY SCENT AND GLORIOUSLY SENSUAL, SILKY TEXTURE. THE SCORED FLESH AND DIAMOND BRANDING MAKE A VISUALLY APPEALING DESSERT.

SERVES SIX

INGREDIENTS
250g/9oz/1¼ cups sugar
juice of 6 limes
3 star anise
6 small or 3 medium to large
  mangoes
groundnut (peanut) oil, for brushing

1 Place the sugar in a heavy pan and add 250ml/8fl oz/1 cup water. Heat gently until the sugar has dissolved. Increase the heat and boil for 5 minutes. Cool completely. Add the lime juice and any pulp that has collected in the squeezer. Strain the mixture and reserve 200ml/7fl oz/scant 1 cup in a bowl with the star anise.

2 Pour the remaining liquid into a measuring jug or cup and make up to 600ml/1 pint/2½ cups with cold water. Mix well and pour into a freezerproof container. Freeze for 1½ hours, stir well and return to the freezer until set.

3 Transfer the sorbet mixture to a processor and pulse to a smooth icy purée. Freeze for another hour. Alternatively, make the sorbet in an ice cream maker; it will take about 20 minutes, and should then be frozen for at least 30 minutes before serving.

4 Prepare the barbecue. Pour the reserved syrup into a pan and boil for 2–3 minutes, or until thickened a little. Leave to cool. Cut the cheeks from either side of the stone (pit) on each unpeeled mango, and score the flesh on each in a diamond pattern. Brush with a little oil. Heat a griddle on the grill rack over hot coals. Lower the heat a little and grill the mango halves, cut-side down, for 30–60 seconds until branded with golden grill marks.

5 Invert the mango cheeks on individual plates and serve hot or cold with the syrup drizzled over and a scoop or two of the sorbet. Decorate with star anise.

COOK'S TIP
If this dessert is part of a larger barbecue meal, cook the mangoes in advance using a griddle set over the first red hot coals. Set aside until ready, and serve cold.

Energy 250kcal/1068kJ; Protein 1.3g; Carbohydrate 64.7g, of which sugars 64.2g; Fat 0.3g, of which saturates 0.2g; Cholesterol 0mg; Calcium 40mg; Fibre 3.9g; Sodium 6mg.

FRUIT SKEWERS <u>WITH</u> LIME CHEESE

GRILLED FRUITS MAKE A FINE FINALE TO A BARBECUE, AND ARE ESPECIALLY GOOD COOKED ON LEMON GRASS SKEWERS, WHICH GIVE THE FRUIT A SUBTLE LEMON TANG. THE FRUITS USED HERE MAKE AN IDEAL EXOTIC MIX, BUT ALMOST ANY SOFT FRUIT CAN BE SUBSTITUTED.

SERVES FOUR

INGREDIENTS

4 long fresh lemon grass stalks
1 mango, peeled, stoned (pitted) and
 cut into chunks
1 papaya, peeled, seeded and cut
 into chunks
1 star fruit (carambola), cut into
 thick slices and halved
8 fresh bay leaves
freshly grated nutmeg
60ml/4 tbsp maple syrup
50g/2oz/¼ cup demerara (raw) sugar
For the lime cheese
 150g/5oz/⅔ cup curd cheese or
  low-fat soft cheese
 120ml/4fl oz/½ cup double
  (heavy) cream
 grated rind and juice of ½ lime
 30ml/2 tbsp icing (confectioners') sugar

1 Prepare the barbecue. Position a lightly oiled grill rack over the hot coals. Cut the top of each lemon grass stalk into a point with a sharp knife. Discard the outer leaves, then use the back of the knife to bruise the length of each stalk to release the aromatic oils. Thread each stalk, skewer-style, with the fruit pieces, alternating one or two chunks with the bay leaves.

2 To make the lime cheese, mix all the ingredients together in a bowl.

3 Place a piece of foil on a baking sheet. Lay the kebabs on top and sprinkle a little nutmeg over each. Drizzle the maple syrup over and dust liberally with the demerara sugar. Grill for 5 minutes, until lightly charred, basting with the maple syrup from the foil, if necessary. Serve the lightly charred fruit kebabs with the lime cheese.

COOK'S TIP

Only fresh lemon grass will work as skewers for this recipe. It is now possible to buy lemon grass stalks in jars. These are handy for curries and similar dishes, but are too soft to use as skewers.

Energy 360kcal/1508kJ; Protein 7.1g; Carbohydrate 43.4g, of which sugars 43.3g; Fat 19.3g, of which saturates 12g; Cholesterol 50mg; Calcium 98mg; Fibre 3.7g; Sodium 219mg.

GRILLED PAPAYA WITH GINGER

*AMARETTI AND STEM GINGER MAKE A TASTY FILLING FOR PAPAYA, AND THE WARM FLAVOUR OF GINGER
ENHANCES THE SWEETNESS OF THE FRUIT. THE DISH TAKES NO MORE THAN TEN MINUTES TO PREPARE.
DON'T OVERCOOK PAPAYA OR THE FLESH WILL BECOME VERY WATERY.*

SERVES FOUR

INGREDIENTS

2 ripe papayas
2 pieces of stem ginger in syrup,
  drained, plus 15ml/1 tbsp syrup
  from the jar
8 amaretti or other dessert biscuits,
  coarsely crushed
45ml/3 tbsp raisins
shredded, finely pared rind and juice
  of 1 lime
25g/1oz/¼ cup pistachio
  nuts, chopped
15ml/1 tbsp light muscovado
  (brown) sugar
60ml/4 tbsp crème fraîche, plus
  extra to serve

VARIATION
For a subtle change to the filling, use
Greek yogurt and almonds instead of
crème fraîche and pistachio nuts.

1 Prepare the barbecue. Position a grill
rack over the hot coals. Cut the papayas
in half, scoop out their seeds and
discard. Using a sharp knife, slice the
stem ginger into fine pieces the size
of matchsticks.

2 Tip the crushed amaretti biscuits
into a bowl, add the stem ginger
matchsticks and the raisins, and use
your fingers to rub the contents together
into a rough, dry crumble.

3 Stir in the lime rind and juice, and
two-thirds of the nuts, then add the
sugar and the crème fraîche. Mix well.

4 Place each papaya half on a piece of
double-thickness foil. Fill the halves
with the amaretti mixture and drizzle
with the ginger syrup. Sprinkle with the
remaining nuts and close up the foil.
Place on the grill rack over hot coals
and cook for about 25 minutes, or until
tender. Serve with extra crème fraîche.

Energy 292kcal/1228kJ; Protein 3.6g; Carbohydrate 44.6g, of which sugars 35.7g; Fat 12.3g, of which saturates 5.7g; Cholesterol 17mg; Calcium 84mg; Fibre 4.2g; Sodium 127mg.

FRUIT WEDGES WITH GRANITAS

THESE WATERMELON AND ORANGE GRANITAS ARE PERFECT FOR A HOT SUMMER'S DAY AND IDEAL TO FINISH A MEAL. PREPARE THEM IN ADVANCE BUT MAKE SURE THEY ARE NICE AND SLUSHY WHEN READY TO SERVE. FRESH PINEAPPLE, MANGO AND BANANA GRILL QUICKLY AND MAKE A GREAT CONTRAST.

SERVES SIX TO EIGHT

INGREDIENTS
 1 pineapple
 1 mango
 2 bananas
 45–60ml/3–4 tbsp icing
  (confectioners') sugar
For the watermelon granita
 1kg/2¼lb watermelon, seeds removed
 250g/9oz/1¼ cups caster
  (superfine) sugar
 150ml/¼ pint/⅔ cup water
 juice of ½ lemon
 15ml/1 tbsp orange flower water
 2.5ml/½ tsp ground cinnamon
For the spiced orange granita
 900ml/1½ pints/3¾ cups water
 350g/12oz/1¾ cups sugar
 5–6 cloves
 5ml/1 tsp ground ginger
 2.5ml/½ tsp ground cinnamon
 600ml/1 pint/2½ cups fresh
  orange juice
 15ml/1 tbsp orange flower water

1 To make the watermelon granita, purée the watermelon flesh in a blender. Put the sugar and water in a pan and stir until dissolved. Bring to the boil, simmer for 5 minutes, then cool.

2 Stir in the lemon juice, orange flower water and cinnamon, then beat in the watermelon purée. Pour the mixture into a bowl; place in the freezer. Stir every 15 minutes for 2 hours and then at one-hour intervals so that the mixture freezes but remains slushy.

3 To make the spiced orange granita, heat the water and sugar together in a pan with the cloves, stirring until the sugar has dissolved, then bring to the boil and boil for about 5 minutes. Leave to cool and stir in the ginger, cinnamon, orange juice and orange flower water.

4 Remove the cloves, then pour the mixture into a bowl and cover. Freeze in the same way as the granita, above.

5 Prepare the barbecue. Position a lightly oiled grill rack over the hot coals. Peel, core and slice the pineapple. Peel the mango and cut the flesh off the stone (pit) in thick slices. Peel and halve the bananas. Sprinkle the fruit with icing sugar and grill for 3–4 minutes over high heat until slightly softened and lightly browned. Arrange the fruit on a serving platter and scoop the granitas into dishes. Serve immediately.

Energy 433kcal/1848kJ; Protein 2g; Carbohydrate 111.8g, of which sugars 111.2g; Fat 0.7g, of which saturates 0.2g; Cholesterol 0mg; Calcium 71mg; Fibre 1.6g; Sodium 16mg.

MELON WITH GRILLED STRAWBERRIES

SPRINKLING THE STRAWBERRIES WITH A LITTLE SUGAR, THEN GRILLING THEM, HELPS BRING OUT THEIR FLAVOUR. SERVE THIS DELICIOUS FAT-FREE DESSERT ON ITS OWN OR WITH A SCOOP OF THE TANGY, VIRTUOUS LEMON SORBET FEATURED A LITTLE LATER IN THIS CHAPTER.

SERVES FOUR

INGREDIENTS
  115g/4oz/1 cup strawberries
  15ml/1 tbsp icing
    (confectioners') sugar, plus extra
    for dusting
  ½ cantaloupe melon

1 Soak four wooden skewers for 40 minutes. Meanwhile, scoop out the seeds from the half melon using a spoon, and discard them. Using a sharp knife, remove and discard the skin, then cut the flesh into wedges and arrange on a serving plate.

2 Prepare the barbecue. Hull the strawberries and cut them in half. Arrange the fruit in a single layer, cut-side up, on a baking sheet and dust with the icing sugar.

3 Thread the strawberry halves onto skewers and place on a grill rack over a high heat. Grill for 3–4 minutes or until the sugar starts to bubble and turn golden. Remove from the skewers and scatter over the melon slices, dusting with the remaining icing sugar.

COOK'S TIPS
• If possible, place the skewered strawberry halves in a wire basket over the grill rack.
• Remove the strawberries from the heat as soon as the sugar starts to bubble. If left to burn, it will ruin the flavour.

Energy 46kcal/197kJ; Protein 1g; Carbohydrate 10.9g, of which sugars 10.9g; Fat 0.2g, of which saturates 0g; Cholesterol 0mg; Calcium 32mg; Fibre 1.6g; Sodium 12mg.

BAKED BANANAS <u>WITH</u> ICE CREAM

BANANAS, BAKED UNTIL SOFT, MAKE THE PERFECT PARTNER FOR DELICIOUS VANILLA ICE CREAM TOPPED WITH A TOASTED HAZELNUT SAUCE. THIS IS A QUICK AND EASY DESSERT, WHICH IS SURE TO BE ESPECIALLY POPULAR WITH CHILDREN.

SERVES FOUR

INGREDIENTS
    4 large bananas
    15ml/1 tbsp lemon juice
    4 large scoops of vanilla ice cream
For the sauce
    25g/1oz/2 tbsp unsalted
      (sweet) butter
    50g/2oz/½ cup hazelnuts, toasted
      and roughly chopped
    45ml/3 tbsp golden (light corn) syrup
    30ml/2 tbsp lemon juice

1 Prepare the barbecue. Position a grill rack over the hot coals. Brush the bananas with the lemon juice and wrap each banana individually in a double thickness of foil. Grill the bananas for 20 minutes.

2 Meanwhile, make the sauce. Melt the butter in a small pan on the grill rack. Add the hazelnuts and cook gently for 1 minute. Add the syrup and lemon juice and heat, stirring, for 1 minute more.

3 To serve, slit each banana open with a knife and open out the skins to reveal the tender flesh. Transfer to serving plates and serve with scoops of ice cream. Pour the sauce over.

Energy 413kcal/1729kJ; Protein 6g; Carbohydrate 53.5g, of which sugars 49.6g; Fat 19.9g, of which saturates 8.6g; Cholesterol 32mg; Calcium 103mg; Fibre 2.2g; Sodium 115mg.

CRANBERRY AND APPLE SPRITZER

DON'T FORGET TO LOOK AFTER THE NON-DRINKERS AT YOUR PARTY — ALL TOO OFTEN THEY'RE LEFT WITH JUST THE MIXERS, FIZZY DRINKS OR TAP WATER. THIS COLOURFUL, ZINGY COOLER COMBINES TANGY CRANBERRIES WITH FRESH JUICY APPLES AND A SUBTLE, FRAGRANT HINT OF VANILLA.

MAKES SIX TO EIGHT GLASSSES

INGREDIENTS
6 red eating apples
375g/13oz/3½ cups fresh or frozen
   cranberries, plus extra to decorate
45ml/3 tbsp vanilla syrup
ice cubes
sparkling mineral water

COOK'S TIP

To make vanilla syrup, heat a vanilla pod (bean) with 50g/2oz/¼ cup sugar and 30ml/2fl oz water in a pan until the sugar dissolves. Simmer for 5 minutes then leave to cool.

1 Quarter and core the apples then cut the flesh into pieces small enough to fit through a juicer. Push the cranberries and apple chunks through the juicer. Add the vanilla syrup to the juice and chill until ready to serve.

2 Pour the juice into glasses and add one or two ice cubes to each. Top up with sparkling mineral water and decorate with extra cranberries, threaded on to cocktail sticks (toothpicks). Serve immediately.

Energy 51kcal/218kJ; Protein 0.3g; Carbohydrate 13.1g, of which sugars 13.1g; Fat 0.1g, of which saturates 0g; Cholesterol 0mg; Calcium 5mg; Fibre 1.6g; Sodium 17mg.

GRAPEFRUIT AND RASPBERRY COOLER

MAKE PLENTY OF FRESHLY JUICED BLENDS LIKE THIS GORGEOUS COMBINATION AND YOUR GUESTS WILL KEEP COMING BACK FOR MORE. GRAPEFRUIT AND RASPBERRY JUICE MAKE A GREAT PARTNERSHIP, PARTICULARLY IF YOU ADD A LITTLE CINNAMON SYRUP TO COUNTERACT ANY TARTNESS IN THE FRUIT.

MAKES EIGHT TALL GLASSES

INGREDIENTS
1 cinnamon stick
50g/2oz/¼ cup caster
   (superfine) sugar
4 pink grapefruits
250g/9oz/1½ cups fresh or
   frozen raspberries
wedge of watermelon
crushed ice
borage flowers, to decorate (optional)

COOK'S TIP

Make non-alcoholic drinks more interesting by dressing them up with extra fruits and decorations.

VARIATIONS

Serve other stirrers such as cinnamon sticks, or provide sugar stirrers so guests can sweeten their drinks to suit their own personal preference.

1 Put the cinnamon stick in a small pan with the sugar and 200ml/7fl oz/scant 1 cup water. Heat gently until the sugar has dissolved, then bring to the boil and boil for 1 minute. Reserve to cool.

2 Cut away the skins from the pink grapefruits. Cut the flesh into pieces small enough to fit through a juicer funnel. Juice the grapefruits and raspberries, and pour into a small glass jug (pitcher).

3 Remove the cinnamon from the syrup and add the syrup to the grapefruit and raspberry juice in the jug.

4 Carefully slice the watermelon into long thin wedges and place in eight tall glasses. Half-fill the glasses with the crushed ice and sprinkle with borage flowers, if you like. Pour over the pink fruit juice and serve immediately with plenty of napkins to allow your guests to eat the watermelon wedges.

Energy 57kcal/240kJ; Protein 1.1g; Carbohydrate 13.4g, of which sugars 13.4g; Fat 0.2g, of which saturates 0g; Cholesterol 0mg; Calcium 30mg; Fibre 1.8g; Sodium 4mg.

INDEX